Becoming an influential leader isn't a mystery or the result of lucky breaks. In *Kick Some Glass*, leadership experts and practitioners Jennifer Martineau and Portia Mount share research-based, actionable practices to help women build the self-clarity, intention, and agency they require to become the leaders they aspire to be—now.

—Lisa Kay Solomon, Chair, Transformational
Practices and Leadership, Singularity University,
and coauthor of *Moments of Impact*
and *Design a Better Business*

Developing and retaining leaders is the lifeblood of any successful organization. *Kick Some Glass* delivers valuable insights for women, as well as men who are seeking to support and develop women in leadership roles.

—Cutler Dawson, Vice Admiral, US Navy (Ret.),
President/CEO, Navy Federal Credit Union

As a technology and women's advocate, I believe *Kick Some Glass* is the new operating system of a singular movement. Jennifer and Portia's book will help us install the code and integrate it into our journey as changemakers, global shapers, and emerging leaders.

—Tsegga S. Medhin, President, North
Carolina Chapter, UN Women

This is the book I've been waiting for all my career(s)! Relevant research, insightful interviews with diverse leaders, practical quizzes, and an inclusive online community to cocreate leadership futures.

—Amanda Ellis, Executive Director,
Hawaii and Asia-Pacific, Julie Ann Wrigley
Global Institute of Sustainability, Arizona
State University, and former New Zealand
Ambassador to the United Nations

This is one of those rare books that successfully engages the reader by sharing the latest research through stories, tips, and questions. It will help all women think more deeply and strategically about what success means to them in the workplace and in life.

—Dr. Susan R. Madsen, Orin R. Woodbury
Professor of Leadership and Ethics, Woodbury
School of Business, Utah Valley University

Kick Some Glass validates everything I have learned and experienced pursuing my passion to empower women and balance the voice of leadership worldwide. Thank you, Jennifer and Portia, for identifying the barriers and opportunities that women face to become leaders. Leadership is a journey fulfilled when we can live it authentically.

—Andrea Conner, President,
ATHENA International

A must-read, *Kick Some Glass* provides rich, practical advice for women striving to do more as leaders. Jennifer Martineau and Portia Mount bring deep professional and personal experiences and combine this with CCL expertise to create a powerhouse of advice for women.

—Sara King, Principal, Optimum Insights, Inc.,
and coauthor of *Discovering the Leader in You*

A powerfully smart and compassionate evidence-based playbook for leadership and life. Whether your glass ceiling is in your job, your industry, your cultural experiences, or your mindset, this book can help you break through with its insightful stories, sound data, actionable advice, and practical exercises.

—Dr. Brenda Wilkins, Cofounder
and President, SoulPowered

KICK SOME GLASS

10 WAYS
WOMEN SUCCEED
AT WORK
ON THEIR OWN TERMS

JENNIFER W. MARTINEAU
PORTIA R. MOUNT

New York Chicago San Francisco Athens London Madrid
Mexico City Milan New Delhi Singapore Sydney Toronto

1 2 3 4 5 6 7 8 9   QVS   23 22 21 20 19 18

ISBN   978-1-260-12140-7
MHID   1-260-12140-2

e-ISBN   978-1-260-12141-4
e-MHID   1-260-12141-0

Library of Congress Cataloging-in-Publication Data

Names: Martineau, Jennifer, author. | Mount, Portia, author.
Title: Kick some glass: 10 ways women succeed at work on their own terms / Jennifer Martineau, Portia Mount.
Description: 1 Edition. | New York : McGraw-Hill Education, 2018.
Identifiers: LCCN 2018027541| ISBN 9781260121407 (hardback) | ISBN 1260121402
Subjects: LCSH: Women--Employment. | Career development. | Self-actualization (Psychology) | Success--Psychological aspects. | BISAC: BUSINESS & ECONOMICS / Leadership.
Classification: LCC HD6053 .M367 2018 | DDC 650.1--dc23 LC record available at https://lccn.loc.gov/2018027541

McGraw-Hill Education books are available at special quantity discounts to use as premiums and sales promotions or for use in corporate training programs. To contact a representative, please visit the Contact Us pages at www.mhprofessional.com.

CONTENTS

To our mothers,

Ellen Fleming Wells and Barbara Morrow Williams,

the women who brought us into this world and

raised us to be glass-kicking women

PREFACE

When we conceived *Kick Some Glass*, we were on the precipice of something we never thought we'd see in our lifetime. The United States seemed poised to elect its first woman president. (Note: This isn't about politics—it's about gender.) But after the historic election and Hillary Clinton's loss, we wondered how long it would be before another woman comes so close to being elected president of the United States.

After the election, more than five million women (and men) took to the streets around the world to march on behalf of women's rights. While this march, especially in the United States, was largely in reaction to the election of Donald J. Trump, we like to think that the election awakened something that had been dormant for a long time: women stepping forward to be visible and reclaim their voice in society. It was truly an exhilarating moment that continues to this day.

Regardless of her loss, Hillary Clinton's run meant something in the larger context of women's leadership. Increasingly, men and women were asking tough questions about why there weren't more women in leadership positions across all aspects of public life. Were women opting out? Being held back? Holding themselves back?

WHERE ARE ALL THE WOMEN LEADERS?

Part of the answer to those questions came in a wave of news about the toxic conditions women were experiencing in the workplace. As we looked at the broad themes in popular media, we saw something interesting. Women were speaking up more often and in greater numbers about their experiences with workplace sexual harassment and the difficulties of rising to and staying in positions of power. One of the earliest high-profile stories was that of Silicon Valley executive Ellen Pao, who brought a sexual harassment suit against her former employer, venture capital firm Kleiner Perkins. Pao's story was the first of what would become a floodgate of highly visible women willing to risk their careers to expose the seedy underbelly of the hostile work environments they endured. Companies run by men where women were either not present or in subservient roles meant women were completely absent from leadership roles where they could shape the culture. The dam was breaking.

One by one, the stories emerged—first a trickle and then a flood. Management teams and boards of directors scrambled to contain the fallout. As public and shareholder pressure mounted, male executives and board members resigned their positions. But the flood rolled on, and the #MeToo movement came with it.

Originally conceived by Tarana Burke, Me Too was a program to empower women and girls of color who experienced sexual assault, exploitation, and abuse. A decade later, the hashtag #MeToo was reborn online when actresses used it to share their stories of being sexually harassed and assaulted by media and entertainment executives. The #MeToo movement revealed deep-rooted misogyny in those industries and eventually spread to include media, political life, and all kinds of other workplaces. Women around the world from all walks of life came forward with often harrowing, graphic stories. The root causes of the toxic culture that allowed these terrible acts are many, but it's clear that a lack of diversity and women in leadership positions are among them. As the stories continued, we kept asking ourselves, would having more women in positions of power make a difference?

The answer seems obvious if you look at the data. In spite of being 50 percent of the workforce, women continue to be underrepresented in the highest leadership roles. There is still work to be done. Women are still not represented on boards. According to the *New York Times* Upshot column, there are more men on corporate boards named John, Robert, William, or James than there are women on boards, period. Women are also underrepresented in the C-suite. While the number is slowly growing, according to *Forbes* magazine women represent just 6.4 percent of CEOs in the Fortune 500.

But we are finally having honest conversations about the glass ceiling, that phenomenon where women make it to senior roles only to be denied the top spot. We are discovering the language of unconscious bias as it relates to the glass ceiling—when decisions are made without malice that nonetheless prevent women from ascending to senior leadership roles. We are learning that when some women have reached that top spot, it is often when a company or organization was performing its worst. Women often were given opportunities during these moments, only to be in those roles a short time and not necessarily go on to more prominent stable leadership roles afterward. Call it the glass cliff.[1]

THE CLEAR MESSAGE: WE NEED MORE WOMEN LEADERS

We need more women board members and CEOs. We need women in all walks of political life. We need women out front on the most important issues of the day, be it climate change, reproductive rights, education, or social justice reform. We need more women leading public, private, and nonprofit organizations. We need more women to step up and claim the mantle of leadership. And we need the partnership of men and organizations that understand the importance of having a more diverse body of leadership in all of our institutions.

With this as our backdrop, we dove with fierce urgency into our mission: write a book that challenged women to *go hard* after their personal and professional goals by aligning their values and intentions with meaningful action. We know from our research at the Center for Creative Leadership that when you align deep self-awareness with assessment, challenge, and support, profound, lasting change happens.

Unlike other career advice books, our intent isn't to "fix" you. Rather, we want to help you understand the barriers in your way and to share practical, actionable advice to overcome those barriers. We don't give you our opinions about what you can do, but instead we pass on advice backed by the latest research. We also share stories of leaders whose experiences illustrate different ways to put that advice into action. We include the advice of men who we believe bring rich insight that women need to hear. Too often, the voices of men are missing in discussions about advancement for women. Their voices are crucial to our conversations about and movement toward gender parity in the workplace and society. We also challenge ourselves and those reading the book to pay it forward and work more diligently on behalf of girls. We were shocked and disheartened by the data that showed that girls begin to step away from leadership roles as early as in grade school. We can't accept this. Every girl should have the opportunity to fully embrace her authentic self and step into her own leadership power.

We were deeply aware of race and class as we wrote this book. We don't pretend to resolve or adequately address these issues. The realities in the differences of the lived lives of women of color from white women, women in poverty from those in privilege, or women identifying their gender in more fluid versus traditional terms can't be overstated. Intersectionality is a critical issue, and modern feminism is grappling with this as women try to understand the role that race, class, and, increasingly, gender identity play in access and visibility in public life. These issues often dictate who gets a voice and who is considered credible. I (Portia) am African American, and I (Jennifer) come from European ancestors who immigrated to America many generations ago. We approached the writing of *Kick Some Glass* knowing that our experiences in the workplace are dramatically different. Yet while there are stark differences, there are also similarities we all experience as women. This is far too much to cover in a book, so it's our intention to have these discussions in online forums, as well as in our talks and speeches.

We conducted dozens of interviews with accomplished women and men. Some came from blue-collar backgrounds, others were first-generation children of immigrants, and others lived in multiple parts of the world in their youth. They were of many races and backgrounds. Each interview we conducted with these extraordinary leaders was a gift. We also mined thousands of pages of research from our CCL colleagues around the world, as well as from scholars, journalists, and thought leaders with a variety of perspectives. Our conclusion? There is a rich body of work that can help women and the organizations they work for support women's leadership. Our goal is to use the platform of *Kick Some Glass* and the online community to amplify what is known, make it accessible for a very large number of women around the world, and use it to inspire application and more research.

On a deeply personal note, writing *Kick Some Glass* challenged and changed us as wives, mothers, and professionals. During the writing of this book my husband, David, and I (Portia) expanded our family through adoption, an unexpected blessing after experiencing years of infertility. Suddenly, we were thrown back into diaper changes, potty training, and learning to live life with a toddler. I had to adjust to being a working mother to two children, which brought with it a host of changes and logistical challenges. One of those big changes was helping my young son, Gideon, transition from being an only child to being a big brother to his new little sister, Collye Sue. As if adding a new family member were not enough, late into writing the book, I received an incredible job offer. I agonized over leaving my leadership role at CCL, where my career had blossomed for over a decade. I also felt conflicted about taking a new job, having just added a new baby to the family. It was after reflecting on a deep discussion I had with a CEO during an interview for this book that I realized it was exactly the kind of opportunity I needed to take. I was ready. In late 2017 I made the leap and accepted a newly created role as vice president and global leader of strategic marketing at Ingersoll Rand, a global manufacturing company.

I (Jennifer), a mother to three grown children, experienced my own changes during the writing of *Kick Some Glass*. My husband, Jim, and I were about to become empty nesters, which meant a shift in family dynamics. With Sarah in the early stages of her career and getting married, Christopher finishing college and looking ahead to law school, and Grace beginning college, the adventure of considering the next phase of our own personal and professional lives was both exciting and a bit intimidating. Around the time of the publication of *Kick Some Glass*, I will celebrate my twenty-fifth year at CCL, where I started as a young researcher and am now a member of the executive team. My thoughts have turned to my legacy at CCL. While I'm nowhere near retiring, I kept asking myself where I wanted to leave my mark at CCL. The answer is clear. *Kick Some Glass* is part of a larger work of research on women's leadership. Together with an incredible team of CCL researchers and practitioners around the world, we are examining how women can lead successfully and what organizations need to do to enable more women leaders to succeed and more young girls to fully realize their leadership potential. The work on *Kick Some Glass* energized me to catalyze this powerful group of women and men to lend its trusted expertise to the globally increasing momentum to put more women into leadership roles.

We hope this book helps you on your journey to realizing your career and life goals. We hope the stories and grounded advice spur you to take action and keep you motivated even when the going gets tough. As we know from experience, there is no right or wrong way to manage your career. You may aspire to be a CEO or not. You may decide that your path is that of an entrepreneur rather than of a corporate executive. You may decide that you want to lead in a school system or a nonprofit organization. You may be ready to run for public office. That's all great! Our hope is that you'll use the lessons and information in this book to be the absolute best version of yourself that you can be. The important thing is that you create your path to lead where you are most energized and can make a difference in the world. We hope our book will give you the courage to leap, even if the net looks very far away. Your family, your organization, your community, and *you* will be better for the steps you take to be your true authentic self.

A final thought: if this book moves you, makes you think, or challenges you in ways you didn't expect, let us know. Share what you are learning, what you're facing, how you're coping, how you're winning. We want to hear from you. You can reach us through the companion website for this book, www.kicksomeglass.com, or find Portia on Twitter @portiarmount or Jennifer @LeadershipCCL.

Let's *Kick Some Glass*!

ACKNOWLEDGMENTS

Kick *Some Glass* would not have become a reality without the significant contributions of other people. It is with deep gratitude and admiration that we recognize them here. First and foremost, we thank John Ryan, president and CEO of the Center for Creative Leadership, for being an unwavering champion for women in leadership. In both our careers and in the many institutions he's served, John has led by example, hiring and promoting women into positions of leadership. John has been a consistent mentor and sponsor to women throughout his career, and we are fortunate to have had the opportunity to work with and learn from him.

We know we are fortunate to be surrounded by people who are passionate about learning and about helping others to develop. Our colleagues have produced most of the research and development programs we've based our book on, and we see this book as a platform to amplify the great work they've done by bringing it together in one place and drawing out its gender-relevant aspects. We humbly and proudly recognize their contributions throughout because our insights—and CCL's ability to make a difference in the development of leadership for women and girls—rest on their efforts and expertise. Our phenomenal colleagues who contribute to the research and practice of developing women and girls include Shannon Bendixen, Phillip Braddy, Patty Burke, Cathleen Clerkin, Gina Eckert, Katya Fernandez, Kate Frear, Emily Hoole, Micela Leis, Jean Leslie, Lynn Miller, Katherine Pappa, Sunil Puri, Marian Ruderman, Laura Santana, Kelly Simmons, Sophia Zhao, and former colleagues Janet Carlson, Sara King, and Patty Ohlott. Not only have we drawn on their existing publications and leadership development designs as we crafted this book, we have also asked questions and stayed up to date on their current work and thinking to include their most cutting-edge insights. Likewise, we have leaned on the work of other colleagues for specific areas of research and practice that, although they may not be gender-focused, provide important information we've used in these pages. They include David Altman, Kristin Cullen-Lester, Jennifer Deal, David Horth, Sharon McDowell-Larsen, Chuck Palus, Nick Petrie, Sarah Stawiski, Elena Svetieva, former colleagues Corey Criswell, Christine Crumbacher, Julia Fernando, Bill Gentry, Ancella Livers, and Phil Willburn, and former CCL governor and executive-in-residence Ilene Wasserman. It is with great humility and gratitude that we thank these colleagues for their dedication to the research and practice of leadership worldwide.

Our thanks go to Mary Jamis, president of M Creative, and the M Creative design team for developing the spectacular creative campaign used to launch the Women's Leadership Experience, the data from which was so valuable for this book. It was Mary who coined the term "kick some glass," which has evolved beyond a creative campaign to a rallying cry that has resonated with women around the world.

We had the great pleasure of interviewing some incredible senior leaders, both women and men, who shared their experiences and insights with us. We didn't focus entirely on the happy and successful stories. We wanted to hear some of the challenges they'd experienced and the lessons they'd learned. They were incredibly willing to be open and transparent with us, and their stories provide beautiful richness to CCL's research and practice. Our deepest gratitude to Abeer Alharbi, Marcia Avedon, Heather Banks, Mary Beth Bardin, April Miller Boise, Dana Born, Jan Capps, Sue Cole, Jabulile Dayton, Cam Danielson, Deb Derby, Chris Ernst, Nelson Fernandez, Stephen Gerras, Michelle Gethers-Clark, Marta Grau, Leslie Joyce, Kalyn Johnson Chandler, Samantha Lomow, Christine Malcolm, Susana Marin, Michael McAfee, Tim Rice, Steve Reinemund, John Ryan, JoAnna Sohovich, Jim Shelton, Susi Takeuchi, Vance Tang, Chaton Turner, Susan Tardanico, Joan Tao, Josephine Teo, Kecia Thomas, Peter Thonis, and Chuck

Wallington. We also interviewed numerous other executives who did not wish to be named. We are grateful to them for sharing their stories.

Anyone who has written a book knows that the authors are only one part of the team. We are fortunate to have a stellar editorial team working with us. Peter Scisco was the lead editor of *Kick Some Glass* and was with us from the first moments we had the idea for the book. Pete helped us to shape the concept, write a proposal, find our great publishing partner, McGraw-Hill, and create and stay on track with our writing plan and worked with us through multiple rounds of editing and revision. He encouraged us when we got stuck or frustrated and had patience with us, even through the times he probably wondered if these two busy executives would meet their deadlines. Pete, we are forever indebted. We also engaged the support of Elaine Biech, a member of CCL's board of governors and a prolific writer in her own right, to help in the developmental editorial phase. Elaine's editing and recommendations challenged and supported us in pulling the chapters together into a tighter whole. Shaun Martin joined the editorial team as we were nearing the final stages and gave us an additional set of eyes. Kelly Lombardino and Susan Turregano assisted us as the manuscript entered the production phase and served as our expert guides to make the book a successful product. Finally, our editorial team at McGraw-Hill, led by executive editor Casey Ebro, helped us to shape *Kick Some Glass* from our initial proposal through the end product to be the kind of book we wanted it to be—one that will ultimately change the dynamics for women in leadership, resulting in organizations having more women in senior leadership roles to provide their diverse influence.

We are both fortunate to have had so many incredible mentors and sponsors in our lives who supported us during the most challenging and difficult times in our careers. They helped us become the professionals we are today. And we are both blessed to have the full support of our families. They helped us become the women we are today.

JENNIFER THANKS

My journey as a woman leader began in earnest a decade ago as part of my exploration of what was next for me. During this time, I began to learn about the uniqueness I bring as a woman leader and the ways in which I have either been held back or have held myself back. I learned about the incredibly courageous and glass-kicking women on both sides of my ancestry, and stand in awe of the norm-challenging directions they chose. The network of champions who have challenged and supported me since then include my coaches Sara King, John McGuire, and Brenda Wilkins, my spiritual director and friend, Deacon Mike Martini, my mother-in-law, Judy Martineau, who raised my remarkable husband, my brother-in-law Dan Martineau, my partner in crime, Portia Mount, and my amazing CCL colleagues Renée Hultin, David Altman, Emily Hoole, Lynn Fick-Cooper, Bill Pasmore, and Sunil Puri. My mom and dad, Ellen and Herb Wells, set a strong example for my brothers, Richard and David, and me, motivating us to do our best, get educated, and live good lives. Thank you, Mom, Dad, Richard, and David, for loving me through thick and thin. I finally got the sisters I wanted through marriage. My sisters-in-law have kept me grounded, made me laugh, challenged me, and inspired me—exactly what strong and powerful women do for each other. Thank you, Kate Adams, Elaine Martineau, Kathy Runde Martineau, Kristian Martineau, Stacy Martineau, Suzy Rook, Lois Wells, and Lyn Wells. My longtime friend Dawn Swanson completes this wonderful group of sisters. Finally, I cannot thank my family enough. Sarah, Christopher, Grace, and our new son-in-law, Chase Coble—you were patient and encouraging during those weekends and vacations when I was writing rather than hanging out with you. Thank you for being willing to listen to the challenges I was having and helping me work through them, and thank you for loving your imperfect mom (BAB ☺). Dad and I are so very proud of the kind, honest, strong adults you've become. Finally, how do I begin to thank the most important person in my life?

Jim, I honestly don't know how I've been so blessed to have you as my husband and partner. You say you knew what you were getting into when we married at 22, but we had no idea where this road of ours would take us. Thank you for traveling it beside me. I love you.

PORTIA THANKS

Thank you to my amazing sister and best friend, Cynthia Benin Lemus. Sisters always stick together! My life is a testimony to powerful women friendships. I am grateful to my longtime mentor and sponsor Jan Kreamer, who saw my potential early on. Thank you to my dearest friend Lily Kelly-Radford, who helped me get into business school and always gave me ground truth even when I wasn't ready to receive it but needed to hear it; Mona Edwards, whose keen political insight and quiet wisdom taught me the importance of listening; and Susan Tardanico, who picked me up when I was feeling unsure and kicked me in the ass when I felt like slacking off. Thank you also to my wonderful friends Diane Beecher, Karen Stewart, Valencia Macon, Shon Gilmore, and Kristen Hairston for always providing advice and encouragement throughout my career. My gratitude goes out to my former CCL colleagues Jennifer Martineau (my partner in crime), Renée Hultin, Brad Shumaker, Hamish Madan, Dave Altman, Jeff Howard, Jeff Anderson, Susan Smith, and Mike Burger. Thank you to the wonderful mothers of the Winston-Salem Chapter of Jack and Jill of America. The community of support you provide is immeasurable. Thank you to my mom and dad, Paul and Barbara Williams, who always supported my dreams and aspirations and taught me resilience and tenacity in the face of adversity. I know my late brother, Bartholomew Williams, who was an incredible writer in his own right, would be proud of me. He was never far from my mind as I wrote, and I miss him every day. I am grateful to my incredible nanny Eva Santos, who kept the house going and kids fed and occupied during the many nights and weekends I was writing into the wee hours of the morning. A huge thank you to my son, Gideon, and our newest little addition, daughter Collye Sue, who often brought toys, treats, hugs, and welcome distractions to my home office during long writing sessions. Thank you to my sisters-in-law Marsha Mount and Grace Huxtable-Mount and my brothers-in-law Jason Mount and Nelson Lemus. You all are rock solid, and I am so fortunate to have you as family! Thank you to Dr. Carlton Eversley and the congregation of Dellabrook Presbyterian Church. This small but mighty church has been such an incredible support to the Mount family during times of great joy and great sorrow. Finally, a huge thanks to my husband, Dr. David Mount. You are an amazing husband and father. You bring so much wisdom and purpose to my life. I am so very blessed, and I thank you for always supporting me and making me better. I love you.

INTRODUCTION

What is the measure of success? The answer, frankly, isn't important. And the question is misguided. So try this: How do *you* measure your success? For midcareer women, an answer can prove elusive. Cultural expectations, structural impediments, undervalued responsibilities—all of these things and others set invisible boundaries to define performance, acceptance, behavior, and success for women in the workplace. But those barriers aren't really invisible. They are made of glass. We can see through them to the rewards on the other side, but we can't easily claim those rewards as our own. We are here to tell you, kick down that glass! Set your own measures of success. Create the rewards you want from a life you love.

That's why we wrote this book. When we set out, we made three key decisions. First, we would expand the *Kick Some Glass* message beyond the book and onto the web at www.kicksomeglass .com. Please join us there for more dialogue and discovery. Second, because we were both members of a brilliant organization called the Center for Creative Leadership (CCL), we believe fully in the power of bringing evidence-based research and practice together in search of leadership development. And so we shaped the chapters of this book using the wealth of knowledge and practice of our colleagues at CCL. Our third decision was to interview dozens of successful executive women and men to learn from their experiences. Because we are determined to push the dialogue beyond what "the woman" can do, we've woven together the lessons we learned from our interviews and research about how men and organizations can encourage, support, and coach women to take leadership roles.

Kick Some Glass isn't a 12-step program, a manifesto, or a memoir. It's about revealing who you truly are to help you realize your potential in ways you never thought possible. After all, you are the expert on you. Exercises in the book will help you do the deep inner work you need to create lasting, meaningful, personal, and professional change. You'll get beneath the surface to understand the mental models that manifest in self-sabotaging behaviors, missed opportunities, and fear. You'll reveal the values that will help you truly understand the choices and trade-offs you make daily. You'll learn how to tap into the powerful networks you need to provide support and hold you accountable to help you reach your goals. You'll learn realistic, doable solutions for taking care of yourself that will help you sleep better, crush stress, and maintain optimal health. Throughout, you'll be encouraged to create lasting, deep change within—change that will get you unstuck and help you set your own path toward a success you define for yourself.

Your guide to self-discovery and growth comes through these chapters:

1. Live Your Intention: Career women play multiple roles at work and outside of work, which requires understanding and appreciating the choices and trade-offs you must make. It is about understanding the values that drive you and making conscious choices to feel a sense of control over your life.

2. You Got This! Step into Your Power: This chapter addresses agency, a core theme in CCL's women's leadership research. CCL research also shows that women don't compartmentalize their careers and life—they tend to integrate them. This chapter will discuss how the mental models we hold consciously and unconsciously impact our choices and sometimes cause self-sabotaging behaviors.

3. Success Your Way: There are all kinds of recipes for what makes for a successful life or career. There is no one-size-fits-all solution! This chapter explores what we know

about women and how they advance (or don't) in their careers. We help you come up with your own definition of success, which builds on the value exercise in Chapter 1.

4. Build Your Network of Champions: This chapter deals with the importance of developing a strong support network to provide help and accountability partnership. We discuss the important difference between mentorship and sponsorship and why women tend to get overmentored and undersponsored. You'll diagnose and determine how to build the network that you need most.

5. Beat the Imposter Syndrome: Feeling like impostors and having limiting beliefs about themselves keep women from taking the kinds of risks that lead to personal fulfillment and career advancement. We'll point to data showing that women are less likely than men to "fake it until you make it" and give you ways to explore and overcome your sense of imposter syndrome.

6. Get Fit to Lead: You can't lead effectively if you aren't at your mental and physical best. This chapter shares the research and practice from CCL regarding sleep, fitness, diet, and resilience.

7. Motherhood: Don't Drop Out, Power Down: This chapter explores what happens when motherhood and career collide. We deal with the impact of motherhood on careers and how to juggle both and still be fulfilled. Key to that harmony is understanding that motherhood doesn't mean shelving your career.

8. Redefine Work-Life Balance: This chapter explores what CCL knows about work-life balance (hint: it's not about balance but about integrating your work and life in a way that works for you). Take the WorkLife Indicator assessment on www.kicksomeglass.com/wli.

9. Own the Room! Take Charge of Your Personal Brand: We've all heard that successful leaders need to have executive presence. But what does that mean, and how do you get it? Your presence needs to be consistent with your values and authentic to you. It is less about "looking like" an executive and more about understanding who you are and living that brand—you!

10. Pay It Forward: Girls start opting out of leadership opportunities as early as in elementary school. This chapter focuses on how we redefine leadership so that young girls are more able to see themselves as leaders.

We'll wrap it up with an epilogue that brings it all together and energizes you on your journey to becoming the leader you aspire to be.

Authors' note: For the women and men we interviewed and whose stories appear in this book, we use full names when they are first introduced in each chapter, and then first names after that. With a few exceptions, these individuals agreed to be recognized, and we thank them in the acknowledgments. For those who wished to remain anonymous, we created a pseudonym to identify their stories and thank them anonymously in the acknowledgments.

7

Live Your Intention

*Live as if you'll live forever, but live
each day as if it were your last.*

—Dana Born, Brigadier General, USAF (Ret.),
and Faculty Member and Director,
University School of Public Policy,
Harvard Kennedy School of Government

In this chapter, you will learn:

- What it means to live your intention and design a meaningful life at any stage
- How to identify the underlying values that are at the core of your being
- How to make the choices and trade-offs necessary to fulfill your purpose

areer-oriented women typically go to college or university with an idea of what they want to do "when they grow up." But after several years in the workforce, changes in their role or workplace, or reconsideration of what their ideal role looks like, they may find themselves asking, "What am I doing here?" or "Is this what I want to do?" But not Sue Cole. Sue, retired CEO of a national financial institution, knew what was important to her and went after it—tenaciously—even as her life and values evolved. She began her first "real" job at the age of 16. With her freshly minted driver's license in hand, she drove to a jewelry store in her small southern US town and asked for a job. When the skeptical manager asked why he should hire someone with no prior work experience, Sue replied, "You'll be so glad you did! I will do anything you want me to do. I can sell diamonds, and I can wrap gifts." He hired her on the spot. That job started Sue on a path very different from the one her parents had traveled. Well intentioned and loving, her mother and father worked hard at their teaching and construction jobs, respectively. But at home they didn't emphasize education nor spend much time with their three children.

Sue feels she was born an entrepreneur, and she wanted to do something different, something more than she saw in the adults who surrounded her. She wanted to be independent and self-sufficient. Before she could legally drive, she had started two businesses: a lawn-mowing service and a babysitting service. Later, she worked at various jobs and lived at home when she started college, paying her own way toward a degree she believed would give her the independence and self-sufficiency that drove her. After marrying and finishing her degree, she began a career in the banking industry. Sue and her husband, the love of her life, had two daughters together while she continued a full-time career. As her life expanded, so did her motives—challenge and flexibility became as important for Sue as independence and self-sufficiency.

At work, Sue made decisions based on the flexibility she needed to live her full life as a career woman, wife, and mother. She ruled out taking roles that limited even one of those important areas.

But she didn't shy away from career challenges, which became even more important to her after her children were grown and the demands of being a mom diminished. She took on greater challenges. Then, when her husband was diagnosed with terminal cancer and given six months to live, Sue left her banking career for a part-time role in investments that would allow her to spend time with her husband. The love of her life fought cancer for 11 years. During this time, Sue realized she wasn't enjoying the part-time role but couldn't figure out why—until she realized she needed a more challenging career! So she started her own consulting firm, providing strategy, leadership development, and corporate governance guidance to her clients. Whether facing the demands of work or of home, Sue's core values (challenge, flexibility, independence, and self-sustainability) helped her make decisions that kept her aim true—always moving toward her own evolving definition of what it meant to have a "successful life."

LIVING YOUR INTENTION

Asking themselves how they define a successful life is a luxury that many women live without. When the bills need to be paid, they don't have the opportunity to think about whether what they're doing is what they *really* want to do. If this is true for you, simply asking the question can help you feel more control over your future—even if you aren't able to make a change right now. Asking yourself whether you are doing what you want to be doing can empower you to make small adjustments to your current situation. Those small changes can lead you closer to the future you've always imagined. Life comes fast. Change comes hard. So pause. Give yourself permission to explore the question: What do I really want?

There is both a positive and a negative approach to the question. The negative approach is to say, "I am so far from what I started out doing that I'm on the wrong track—I need to fix it." Pause. What thoughts and feelings does that statement provoke in you? Don't dwell on those thoughts, but compare that reaction to what happens when you adopt a positive approach: "The path I've followed so far isn't what I expected, but I've gained skills and knowledge, formed strong connections with colleagues and peers, and had experiences I would not trade for anything—experiences I would have missed if I'd stayed on my original path. What can I take from my history to help me think about where I'd like to go?"

Susana Marin, general manager of a luxury hotel in Spain, knows this: the most important thing she wants people to say about her is that she's honest and fair. This is the value and intent that drives her: she always speaks the truth, even when she knows she can't always tell the full story depending on her audience or the situation. She shares as much as she can without compromising strategic decisions or an individual's privacy. Another intent also inspires Susana: passion. "I cannot be a leader without being passionate about what I do," she says.

Life is a constant series of choices—even if the choice is to do nothing at all. How you got to where you are might seem unclear with the passage of time, but you can pull back your choices like layers to uncover what drove you to make them. You can reveal the messages that have guided your intentions throughout your life and learn how to redirect messages that don't help you move toward your ideal future. That's what this chapter is all about: creating the life you intended to live. It's never too late to design the life you want.

WHAT'S HOLDING YOU BACK?

You may not know the answer to the question, What's holding me back? The reasons why so many women don't live their intent or purpose vary widely. In their book *Standing at the Crossroads*, Marian Ruderman and Patty Ohlott share what they learned about how senior-level women leaders reached authenticity—an alignment of their values with their actions.[1] Achieving authenticity required those women to be fully aware of their intentional choices to trade one part of their life for another. Four key pressures force women to make those choices: personal expectations, others' expectations, organizational practices, and cultural beliefs and practices. Let's see how those play out in the lives of career-minded women.

Personal Expectations

One important reason we decided to write this book was that we wanted to share lessons we'd learned from our careers and personal lives with the hope that doing so could help other women on their own journeys. In our own stories we can see how our intentions influenced the choices we made. My (Jennifer's) story is a case in point:

After taking a general psychology class in high school, I decided I wanted to be a psychologist. Entering college, my only awareness of the roles psychologists played were as clinical or counseling psychologists. I imagined myself listening to patients' problems, empathizing with them, and helping them find solutions. It all made sense until my sophomore year, when I met a graduate student in the university's industrial and organizational (I/O) psychology program and asked her why she was interested in that particular course of study. She said plainly, "I don't want to work with sick people all day." Bang. If epiphany were a rocket, then that moment hit me like an exploding fireworks factory. I had never considered my future patients to be sick—just in need of help. Having been in counseling myself since then, I believe I was correct—my future patients wouldn't have been sick. I have deep respect for counselors and clinicians, as well as for the people who seek their services. But at the same time, this comment opened my eyes to see the extremes experienced by people in these roles. I realized I wasn't sure this profession was for me. I decided to learn more about I/O psychology to give myself some options. After I took a course from that same graduate student, I realized that there was a lot to like about the work I could do in that field.

From that point forward, my goal became a PhD in I/O psychology. I set my sights on top-tier graduate school programs, studied for the entry exams, worked hard in my college classes, and found an internship that gave me practical experience in I/O work within an organization. One of my roommates at the time who remains a very good friend still reminds me about the sticky notes I put around my room in our apartment with "4.0" (a perfect grade point average) and other messages of goals I wanted to reach so that I could achieve my aim of graduate school.

I achieved that PhD in I/O psychology and began working at the Center for Creative Leadership (CCL) as an entry-level, part-time, temporary researcher. This was an organization I had hoped to work in at some point in my career, presumably after I'd paid my dues somewhere else. What an opportunity! I loved the applied research I was able to do at CCL and envisioned a long career doing this work. In fact, when my husband, who challenges and supports me like no other, asked me a year or so into my time at CCL about my interest in taking on a management role at some point in my career, I told him that I wasn't interested in leading—I wanted to do "the work." My image of the work was applied research that had an impact on leaders and their organizations. Just as research indicates about young girls, I'd never seen myself as a leader. I hadn't chosen to compete for formal roles such as class or service club president when in school, nor project lead roles in graduate school. I didn't yet understand the broader nature of leadership—that we lead by our actions as much as (or more than) by title. When I finally realized that, during my early years at CCL, I recognized that I did play leadership roles when I was younger and that people recognized me for these roles. For example, my teammates selecting me as co-captain of our high school's swim team was one of those indications.

With that realization, I committed myself to leading through whatever role I was playing, regardless of its formal title or position. Indeed, my definition of "the work" has evolved over the years! That change has required me to continuously rediscover my values and intentions and determine how to live them authentically in my life. I did not foresee myself in my current role when I was in graduate school or early in my career—my path has not been what I'd call intentional and planned (more on that later). At times, my professional life has been confusing, frustrating, and fraught with doubt. But I was intentionally open to new opportunities that promised the chance to have a positive impact on leaders, their organizations, and their communities—and by doing that, having a positive impact on our world. Those values and intentions have continued to guide my choices throughout my career.

My story describes some of what holds women back from living their intentions. I made assumptions about leadership roles that kept me from imagining myself in those positions. My expectations dissuaded me from putting myself forward for consideration for those roles. I am not a special case—far from it. Research tells us that women believe they need to be 100 percent qualified to do a job before they take it on, but men are more likely to put themselves forward for new opportunities even if they haven't proven themselves fully capable of taking on more responsibilities.[2]

Fortunately, some men notice when women don't put themselves forward. CCL's president, retired US Navy Vice Admiral John Ryan, worked with and led men and women throughout his Navy career and later as superintendent of the US Naval Academy and chancellor of the State University of New York (SUNY) system. He recognizes that women don't put their hands up quickly enough when a new opportunity comes along, and he encourages them not to hold back. "You don't know how to fly an actual plane when you first get that assignment. You've only flown in simulators up to that point," he says. "You are never really ready for the next job—you haven't done it yet. You have to be ready to learn on the job." John is right: you don't know all the intricacies of flight before you strap into a cockpit for the first time solo. But you have trained in simulators. You know the controls and the physics of flying. My first simulation was a leadership role as co-captain of the swim team. No, it didn't involve all the intricacies of leading people and projects in a global organization. But, looking back,

I see it was practice. Look back on your life for those times you practiced leadership.

Another man we interviewed, Chris, has observed from his diverse leadership roles—in philanthropy, the tech sector, and at a nonprofit organization—a phenomenon in which his female teammates are less likely to step into an opportunity than men are. He attributes it to a system that tells men to "grab the opportunity, you've got a green light, go for it, carpe diem" and says to women, "don't go too fast, are you sure you want to take that step, do you have support from this person or that person?" So how does Chris support his female colleagues with this challenge? He has learned from many years of experience that the best way for him to support his colleagues is to listen to them. "I believe that solving problems is part of my male hardwiring," he says. "But I discovered that the way I could support my teammates best is really to understand their situation, not to solve it." John and Chris both reflect research that shows that women may be hesitant to advocate for themselves.[3] That hesitation can prevent them from living their intention.

Others' Expectations

When we're not hesitating to put ourselves forward, many times we make career decisions based on the expectations that others have of us. One example we see often is based on tension between a women's desire for a professional career and the expectation that women will care for the children. The strength of that expectation can vary among cultures, as we see in attorney Joan Tao's story.

Joan's parents came to the United States from their native Taiwan in the mid-1960s to attend graduate school before Joan was born, which makes Joan a first-generation US citizen. Joan's mother is highly educated for a woman of her generation. Joan's grandmother trained as a pharmacist in Japan, and her grandfather was a doctor. Because both of her grandparents were deeply involved in their family's medical practice, Joan's mother grew up without much involvement from either of them. As a result, she decided to spend more time with her own children when she became a mother. After completing her graduate degree, Joan's mother became a homemaker and was very present in Joan's life.

Joan learned as a young adult that she was expected to "marry up"—to marry someone whose career goals were equal to or higher than hers. When she did meet someone who fit that bill in her parents' eyes, she learned that his parents saw her as too strong—she would not fit their expectations as a future daughter-in-law. Joan felt like she had to downplay her own success to meet the expectations of others, which made her angry.

That relationship didn't work out, and the man Joan eventually met and married didn't define success through others' approval. He supported Joan throughout her career, in law firms and then as corporate counsel. Her mother encouraged her as well but sent mixed messages. She would ask Joan, "Why aren't you home with your kids?" and "Why didn't you marry a man who could facilitate your life as a stay-at-home mother?" Joan's husband, a college professor, took a more active role in parenting than Joan's father (and most fathers in his generation) had. So there was no question in either of their minds whether their children had parental guidance. Sometimes it came from Joan, sometimes from her husband. Their arrangement enabled Joan to pursue her career in law, despite its long hours and frequent travel. But it was certainly not traditional in the way her parents' parenting had been. Nor was it the same choice her mother had made.

Joan's story shows how we can feel pressure to make some of our choices based on the expectations of others (or others can make choices for us)—parents and potential in-laws, for example. Joan's mother's expectation was that Joan must be present for her children in order to be a good mother, and Joan felt burdened by that perception of what parenting looked like. Joan went against her mother's expectations, but they were never far from her mind, and she sometimes felt guilt when she thought she might not be living up to them.

Organizational Practices

To understand what lay behind the shrinking number of women in leadership globally, CCL and the Network of Executive Women (NEW) surveyed over 900 women to learn about the barriers they encounter in the workplace.[4] CCL's researchers Emily Hoole, Jean Brittain Leslie, Shannon Bendixen, Robert Solomon, and Regina Eckert found that conflicting work-life demands are the number one barrier, but the second and third are based on organizational practices. The first of these was *being overlooked and undervalued*, and the second was *being undermined*. We'll explore each separately.

In terms of being overlooked and undervalued, women in the study reported that they are not groomed for leadership positions to the same extent as their male colleagues. They are often excluded from important business conversations, are told they aren't ready for additional responsibility, and do not feel properly acknowledged for their work and contributions.

Leslie Joyce knows how it feels. Self-motivated, confident, and competent, she had risen to the C-suite, having served as chief HR officer of a large global manufacturing company and chief learning officer of a consumer goods company. However, this track record of success was not sufficient to overcome the organizational practices inherent in one company. The prior two companies had strong cultures committed to leadership, diversity, and the advancement of women. This company was different. Here Leslie experienced the perfect storm of bias: she was a woman, leading a staff function, in a struggling company. Though she was well-liked as a person, she was not part of the "in-group" of men who shared a common interest in sports. She led a functional area (a cost center) rather than a business unit (a revenue center). When she wasn't invited to strategic meetings, she showed up anyway and found she was accepted and her input was appreciated. Why wasn't she included? The explanation was that they just hadn't "thought" to include her; they didn't think of her, or her perspective, as "relevant" to the topic. As the person responsible for the people strategy, she believed her perspective was always relevant. Leslie eventually left the company. Her contributions were overlooked and undervalued.

Marta Grau also encountered this barrier when she became responsible for a restructuring at her publishing company. The senior team didn't know exactly where to put the production department, and, sensing an opportunity for growth, Marta asked for the assignment. Marta already had HR responsibilities and had spent her career at that organization in HR. When her boss told her she had no clue about production, Marta said, "You are right—I don't have a clue about production. But no one else on the team does either, and I will learn. I can assure you that I will help the leader of that group and resource it like no one else can because I understand people more than anybody else!" Marta got that assignment, and in two years the group had improved upon all of its success measures—in time, quality, and production. Marta turned a moment when she was undervalued into a high point in her career.

Another set of women in this study—those at middle manager levels—reported being overlooked and undervalued more than women at other career levels. This is *exactly* why we are writing this book! If women at the middle management levels are overlooked and undervalued more than women at other levels, that is a crucial moment in their careers when they need to understand why this is happening and what can be done about it—by them or by others.

The second barrier identified was *being undermined*. Women in the study described having their qualifications routinely questioned, having information withheld from them, and having a boss or superior refuse to support them in their career advancement.

Women in general report these barriers, and women of color report them even more strongly. Women of color also report lower career satisfaction than other women. Interestingly, women of color in this study perceive fewer negative trade-offs to being a senior leader versus white women. For us, these findings raise questions about why women of color report being undermined more and being less satisfied than white women, yet perceive fewer negative trade-offs to being a senior leader. If you are a woman of color, does this sound familiar to you?

This research from CCL and NEW also reveals that women may encounter barriers in organizations that are the result of second-generation or unconscious bias—social stereotypes that people form about groups that are unlike them but about which they are unaware. Common sources of unconscious bias in organizations for women include:

- Traditional images of leadership are associated with qualities that are viewed as male qualities. Thus when people are asked to think about someone with good leadership qualities, they often envision a man rather than a woman.

- Women have few female role models at high levels of leadership. Thus women are less likely to "see" themselves as leaders because they don't see anyone who looks like them in most leadership roles.

- Career paths and work are often defined by or associated with gender. For example, multinational corporations often require expat assignments of their leaders before promoting them. Fewer women than men relocate their families for rotational assignments. Thus fewer women are ascending to senior leadership roles.

- Women are held to higher standards and offered fewer rewards. Almost regardless of the industry, country, or age group, women earn less than men in the same roles. For example, US data reflects that women earn approximately 80 percent of men's earnings on an annual basis.[5] The outlook is even worse for black and Hispanic women, where their earnings fall to 63 percent and 54 percent of men's, respectively.[6] In order to achieve pay on par with a man, a woman would need to work at a higher level of capability than the man. In other words, *doing more and better* for the same pay as a man *doing less and average.*

- Women are not part of the networks that supply information and support to men. When jobs are open, "who you know" is often important. If women are in fewer networks than men and are not in networks that link them to opportunities, they are less likely to be put forward as possible candidates for advancement.

- Women face a double bind of being competent or being liked—but not both. Research bears this out.[7] When men and women are perceived as competent, women are liked less than men. When men and women are liked by others, the women are perceived as being less competent than men.

- The combination of work and home responsibilities is a greater burden for women than for men. Women are typically expected to hold more of the home-care role (whether with regard to aging parents, sick partners, or children), and because organizations and work are often structured on the assumption that there is a partner at home to perform the home-care role, working women face the tension of managing home responsibilities without letting work responsibilities suffer.

You may not be able to influence any or all of these sources of bias in organizations. We share them to help you understand some of what you may be experiencing and to let you know you aren't alone! Later in the chapter, we'll ask you to think about the influence you *do* have—if not to help yourself, then to help other women coming up behind you.

We encountered several examples of unconscious bias when we interviewed senior women leaders. In Joan's case, she planned to work her way up to partner in a law firm, but she realized early in her career that she knew very few women partners. One female partner read her daughter's bedtime stories to her over the phone most nights because she was at the office. Another had made partner with a one-year-old child. Joan asked her how she'd done that, and she answered that she hadn't given birth—her partner had. A third woman at the firm had become partner much later in life. Joan had a hard time imagining herself as a partner in a firm when she saw few women—especially women with children—in those roles.

Jan Capps is a retired CEO of a health foundation and previously the head of HR for a global agribusiness company. Although her own company was supportive of her, she has encountered the challenges of innate bias in organizations that force women—more so than men—to carry the dual burden of career and home-care roles. She told us, "I am struggling with the notion of how women manage families and work. . . . I never felt like there was work-life balance. One of them won each day, and they never balanced on any one day. You have to look at it over a year or 20 years. I struggle with the idea that women take time out from career and can still expect to make it to the top. I don't think that this is very likely. I coach women that, as a leader, you have to depend on people below you to meet deadlines." Observing the work and home tension that many organizations ignore, Jan relies on a metaphor from her agribusiness days. "Hybrid corn is stronger than a single strain for a reason—so is society," she says. In other words, leaders (men or women) are stronger when they build strength in the workplace *and* on the personal front. In the same way, organizations and society are stronger when people build strength in multiple parts of their lives.

Cultural Beliefs and Practices

Cultures have a powerful effect on both an individual's aspirations and limitations. Especially telling is how a particular society envisions a woman's role: Is it mainly family oriented and supportive of the male or husband? Or is it egalitarian, not only allowing but promoting a woman's career in any and every field of work, whether blue collar, white collar, entrepreneurial, or artistic?

Despite her training as a nuclear physicist in Saudi Arabia, Abeer Alharbi knows firsthand the power of cultural limitations. Abeer, who teaches at a university in Riyadh, was born the fifth of 14 children and was the only girl in the home for many years. Abeer's father was an educator and authored a number of books on geography. Abeer helped her father in his work, analyzing his data at the age of 10 and reading his books. Her father discussed the content of those books with her. She admired him and one of her brothers who was working on his PhD. By the time she reached fifth grade, Abeer was already planning for her own PhD. "That was not so common then," she says. She wanted to prove that "women can do stuff." Medical school was her original goal, but her conservative family stopped her from pursuing a career as a physician. Working in a mixed-gender environment was out of the question. While in medical school, Abeer would have to work in hospitals and late at night—conditions deemed inappropriate for a young woman in Riyadh. So although her dream was medicine, Abeer obeyed her family's wishes and chose to go into physics instead.

While the immediate message of limitations came from Abeer's family, it was grounded in much more than that. The limitations she faced came from the cultural beliefs and practices in Saudi Arabia that kept women from participating alongside men in most spaces of life outside of the home. And though Abeer is an example of the small percentage of women who have successfully pursued graduate degrees and professional roles in Saudi Arabia, her ability to practice in her field has not been wide open. After Abeer earned her PhD and completed a Fulbright Fellowship in the United States, she returned to Riyadh and became a professor of nuclear physics at the largest women's university in the world, where students are taught almost exclusively by women faculty. She also served as the dean of development and skills enhancement, responsible for establishing and leading professional development for the faculty and staff at the university. Although she has been challenged and has learned in the roles she's played, Abeer is confident that Saudi Arabia isn't getting the best out of her, yet she is driven to deliver it.

Saudi Arabia began to allow women to drive in 2017, but the beliefs and practices that have long held women from participating fully in the workforce, should they choose, will take years and perhaps generations to evolve. Yet Saudi Arabia is not the only country whose culture presents these types of challenges for women. Based on a 2016 study by Grant Thornton,[8] no country in the world can say that half of its business leadership roles are held by women. Russia came closest with 45 percent of senior management roles held by women; the Philippines and Lithuania each had 39 percent. The United States ranked below 22 of the 36 countries studied, with 23 percent of senior leadership roles held by women, while Japan had the least at 9 percent. So consider the impact of cultural beliefs and practices on your ability to live your intention.

Susana, the luxury hotel general manager we told you about earlier, wanted to be in a luxury hotel GM role from early in her career. To prepare, she worked in all of the hotel's departments to get exposure to everything it takes to run a high-end hotel. She got a job in the sales department at one point, but gave it up to take an operations training opportunity at a large global hotel chain. People told her she was crazy to give up her sales role that would put her on a fast track for growth in that area, but she wanted to be a GM. She knew she would need to learn what it was like to work on the operations teams so that she could lead them. More than once she learned the value of going the extra mile, such as the times she put her shoes back on her swollen feet after a very long day so that she could help her team members who were being asked to clean and change a room very late in the day. Susana put her intentions and values above the expectations of others in achieving her role.

We also told you about Jan, retired health foundation CEO. She was driven by values to solve interesting problems. Jan was a single mother of two for a number of years in her early to mid career and needed to be sure that any opportunity she took would provide the financial support her family needed and enable her children to live a stable life. When Jan was asked if she'd be interested in a new role that would give her a new challenge and more exposure at the corporate level, she saw a problem right away: company headquarters was a 12-hour drive from her family's home. So she solved it. Jan presented a proposal for how she could manage the job by spending three days a week in the headquarters office and two in her hometown office. She gave evidence that showed how her plan would save the organization money—it was cheaper to cover her commuting expenses than to relocate a family of three. Her children stayed with their father most of the nights she was in the headquarters office and remained in their schools, which enabled them to continue their routine. As any frequent traveler can attest, a weekly commute of this distance (even by plane or train) can be draining, on top of an already full and complex life. Yet for Jan, the trade-off was worth it. She could take on a new challenge and meet her family's needs. Jan put her problem-solving skills to work to find space for her values and intentions while fulfilling the needs of the company. In due course, she opened the organization's eyes to new ways of working that benefited both women and men.

As you've seen so far, many times women are making choices about how closely to live their intentions and values. Sometimes there is no question about making choices when values are non-negotiable. Kecia Thomas, a professor of psychology and senior associate dean at a large university, removed herself from consideration for an attractive position after finishing graduate school because the organization recruiting her was one whose products targeted the minority community and played a role in its generally poor health. To work for such a company conflicted with Kecia's social justice values. She rejected an attractive opportunity rather than compromise her beliefs.

Now that you've learned about the many ways that barriers may stand in the way of living your values and intentions, and you've heard from senior women who have struggled through what you may be experiencing, let's start helping you live your intention.

HOW CAN YOU LIVE YOUR INTENTION?

First of all, realize that your purpose and intention may change multiple times during your lifetime. Think about that. Are you doing the very thing you identified as your direction early in life? When you were in your twenties? Even if you are, does that mean it's the right direction for the remainder of your career? We all learn and grow and have the capacity to change. The world around us is ever shifting. And that provides ample opportunities for you to recraft your purpose and intent over and over again. We set out to help you with these three foundational steps in this chapter:

- What it means to live your intention and design a meaningful life at any stage

- How to identify the underlying values that are at the core of your being

- How to make the choices and trade-offs you need to make to fulfill your purpose

To live your intention, you need to know what your intention is. If you're like us, you might not have realized that you need to identify (and re-identify) your purpose many times during your career. We don't know about you, but we certainly didn't know how to do that. We learned pretty quickly that it's not enough to just point yourself in a certain direction. Our advice to you? Don't get anxious. Get started.

Values Explorer Exercise

Values have four key characteristics:

- **They define who you are.** Your values are often what others would say best describes the way you behave and what others can expect from you.

- **Values are rooted in your past.** We often hold similar values to our parents and grandparents, or hold values we formed as children.

- **Values can conflict with one another.** Some of your values may cause tension with other values. Sometimes one of your values trumps another. In that tension is where we learn about what is most important to us.

- **Values are aspirational.** They often inspire us to be more than we are and suggest what we might be. In our best moments we embody our core values.

CCL developed the following Values Explorer exercise to help you explore and understand values in the workplace and in your personal life. It was designed to help you understand who you are deep down— what core values drive your decisions and actions. It can be used by a single individual, a coaching pair, and in small and large groups. It is also available to you on www.valuableleaderproject.com or through the ValueAble Leader Project link on www.kicksomeglass.com.

Instructions

1. Photocopy the values list that follows. Cut on the dotted lines and tape or glue each value and its description to a separate index card to make a set of 44 values cards.

(continued)

VALUES LIST

ACHIEVEMENT
A sense of accomplishment, mastery.

LOYALTY
Faithfulness. Duty. Dedication.

FRIENDSHIP
Close personal relationships with others.

COMMUNITY
To serve and support a purpose that supersedes personal desires. To make a difference.

ADVENTURE
New and challenging opportunities. Excitement. Risk.

PHYSICAL FITNESS
Staying in shape through exercise and physical activity.

HUMOR
The ability to laugh at oneself and life.

COMPASSION
A deep awareness and sympathy for another's suffering.

AFFLUENCE
High income, financial success, prosperity.

TRUSTWORTHINESS
Responsibility. Dependability, reliability, accountability for results.

CHANGE/VARIETY/ABSENCE OF ROUTINE
Work responsibilities, daily activities, or settings that change frequently. Unpredictability.

ACTIVITY
High-pace conditions where work is done rapidly.

ORDER
Respectful of authority, rules, and regulations. A sense of stability, routine, predictability.

HAPPINESS
Finding satisfaction, joy, or pleasure.

COMPETENCE
Demonstrating a high degree of proficiency and knowledge. Showing above-average effectiveness and efficiency at tasks.

AESTHETICS
Appreciation of the beauty of things, ideas, surroundings, personal space, etc.

RECOGNITION
Positive feedback and public credit for work well done. Respect and admiration.

INFLUENCE
Having an impact or effect on the attitudes or opinions of other people. The power of persuasion.

COURAGE
Willingness to stand up for one's beliefs.

AUTHORITY
Position and the power to control events and activities of others.

JUSTICE
Fairness, equality, doing the "right" thing.

ECONOMIC SECURITY
Steady and secure employment. Adequate financial reward. Low risk.

SELF-RESPECT
Pride, self-esteem, sense of personal identity.

KNOWLEDGE
The pursuit of understanding, skill, and expertise. Continuous learning.

FAMILY
Time spent with spouse, children, parents, relatives.

COLLABORATION
Close, cooperative working relationships with group.

ADVANCEMENT
Growth, seniority, and promotion resulting from work well done.

PERSONAL DEVELOPMENT
Dedication to maximizing one's potential.

HELP OTHERS
Helping other people attain their goals. Providing care and support.

COMPETITION
Rivalry, with winning as the goal.

AFFILIATION
Interaction with people. Recognition as a member of a particular group. Involvement. Belonging.

REFLECTION
Taking time out to think about the past, present, and future.

INTEGRITY
Acting in accord with moral and ethical standards. Honesty. Sincerity. Truth.

CREATIVITY
Discovering, developing, or designing new ideas, programs, or things using innovation and imagination. Creating unique formats.

AUTONOMY
Ability to act independently, with few constraints. Self-sufficiency. Self-reliance. Ability to make choices.

SPIRITUALITY
Strong spiritual or religious beliefs. Moral fulfillment.

LOCATION
Choice of a place to live (town, geographic area, etc.) that is conducive to one's lifestyle.

FAME
To become prominent, famous, well known.

BALANCE
Giving proper weight to each area of one's life.

STATUS
Impressing or gaining respect of friends, family, and community by the nature and/or level of responsibility of one's job or by association with a prestigious group or organization.

LOVE
To be involved in close, affectionate relationships. Intimacy.

ENJOYMENT
Fun, joy, and laughter.

CHALLENGE
Continually facing complex and demanding tasks and problems.

WISDOM
Sound judgment based on knowledge, experience, and understanding.

(continued)

2. Sort each of the values into one of five categories, according to how important it is to you: Always, Often, Sometimes, Seldom, and Never Valued. Do your best to distribute them across the five categories, even if you're tempted to put most of them in the Always and Often categories. You will still end up with more in some categories than in others, but push yourself to differentiate the importance each value holds for you. The Never Valued category is particularly important. It holds the values that you would never act upon or demonstrate. You will always make choices to avoid these values.

3. After you finish sorting, look at the values in the Always category. Rank them in order of priority. Rank highest the value you will never compromise. All of the values you retain in the Always category should be nonnegotiable. You ought to align your career choices with them. As you consider whether each of these values is truly nonnegotiable, ask yourself:
   - This value has been important to me in the past, but is it still nonnegotiable?
   - Did I choose this value because I think other people value it or expect it of me, or is it truly something I treasure?
   - What do these values say about the kind of role I want to find or create?
   - Have I ever had a role (or roles) where I was truly able to live these values? What did I love about the role? What did I not love?

   If there are any values you determine are not as nonnegotiable as you first thought, move them to the Often category.

4. Look at your Never Valued category. The values here should be those that you would never consider acting upon. You would make choices that minimized these values. Consider these values by asking yourself questions such as:
   - Would I never want to fulfill these values?
   - What do these values say about the kind of role I want to avoid?
   - Have I ever had a role (or roles) where these values were prioritized? If so, was there anything I liked about the role (or the organization, or the people I worked with)? What did I dislike?

5. The values you've identified as Always valued and Never valued set parameters for how you might think about opportunities you want to seek or create for yourself. Look for opportunities that align with the

Always valued pile and eliminate opportunities that connect to your Never valued pile.

6. As you examine potential opportunities and weigh them against your values, you might spot contradictions. For example, if you placed Family and Status in the Always valued category, you might find it difficult to find opportunities that lead to high status and enable you to devote as much time to your family as you'd like to. There are always choices we must make and trade-offs we must consider.

QUESTIONS FOR REFLECTION

Throughout *Kick Some Glass*, we recommend that you use a journal to respond to questions intended to help you capture and process your thoughts and feelings and to move you along your development journey. Such a journal can be an invaluable tool for developing insight and for growing as a leader.

To get started, reflect on these questions in your journal:

- What can I take from my personal history to help me think about where I'd like to go?

- How have my intentions and my sense of purpose informed the choices I've made in my life?

- What did I learn about myself from the Values Explorer or ValueAble Leader exercise? What surprised me? How have my values shifted over time?

You Got This! Step into Your Power

When you give away your power, you won't get it
back. I've taken that lesson with me in gaining
and becoming responsible for my power.

—Jabu Dayton, Principal, Jabu HR, Inc.

In this chapter, you will learn:

- How to get comfortable with your personal power and understand what it means to live with agency to drive toward your intentions and life aspiration
- How to uncover the conscious and subconscious mental models that may be holding you back from realizing your deepest desires

How do we take control of our lives and drive toward what's truly important to us? It starts with thinking about what really matters to you. It also means not putting others' priorities and needs ahead of your own (a challenge for some women). And it sometimes means saying no to what on the surface may sound right—like the job you're offered that pays well but doesn't fit your values and vision. Live with agency. Make decisions aligned with your priorities and your unique contributions. You can lean in, but if you lean in the wrong direction, you might fall down.

AGENCY: WHAT IT MEANS TO STEP INTO YOUR POWER

The term *agency* was coined by psychologist David Bakan,[1] who described agency as the human desire to control one's life and to excel. Agency motivates us to achieve; it propels us to ask and work for what we want. In many cultures, especially in the West, men are rewarded for showing agency: assertiveness, making the first move, and asking for what they want. Others see those actions as powerful and judge the men who act that way to be good leaders. Displays of agency by women are often cast in a negative light. Attributes such as assertiveness, self-advocacy, and outspokenness are often labeled as bossy, pushy, or unfeminine. (See Chapter 9 for a detailed discussion of this phenomenon.)

Acting with agency doesn't mean running roughshod over others or being arrogant and manipulative. In the CCL book *Standing at the Crossroads*, Marian Ruderman and Patty Ohlott describe it as simply giving voice to your needs and desires and acting on your own behalf.[2] Consider the role of a talent agent who helps an actor find the roles that best match her brand. Don't you wish you had a talent agent? You do. It's you. You need to be your own agent, looking for opportunities that serve your intentions and purpose. We know that without those qualities of self-promotion and assertiveness, women can languish in their careers. They are passed over for promotions, don't get highly desired assignments, and miss out on sponsorship that is so crucial for their growth and career advancement.

Deb Derby avoided those pitfalls by using her agency to keep herself on track.

The president of a national craft and novelty company, whose major customers include Walmart and Target, Deb was the first in her family to attend college. She earned her undergraduate degree from Harvard, followed by a JD/MBA from the University of Notre Dame. When she entered the workforce, she kept a razor-sharp focus on her career pursuits. She rose steadily, from her early days as a financial analyst at Goldman Sachs, to management positions of increasing responsibility at Whirlpool, to executive leadership positions at Toys "R" Us, and, finally, to her current role. Each of those roles expanded her capabilities in different ways. An early stint at a law firm allowed her to work with a senior law partner, who gave her honest (and sometimes brutal) feedback and challenged her to sharpen her communication and analytical skills with each successive brief. He became a lifelong mentor. An employee relations role with Whirlpool exposed her to HR, talent management, and compensation. Her career at Toys "R" Us provided her with her first chance at a senior general management position. With each successive position, Deb looked for opportunities to learn something new and to expand her skill sets into areas where she didn't have prior experience.

There's no doubt that Deb has a ferocious work ethic and an innate curiosity and hunger for knowledge that helped fuel her success. But so did several mentors along the way who helped coach, and, in many cases, sponsor her for positions outside of her areas of expertise. An objective observer might look at her career choices and see someone figuring out what she liked and didn't like to do, and who was willing to take calculated risks to move on when she felt she had mastered the job she was in. Deb acted with profound agency to steer herself toward opportunities that best met her vision for her career and life.

Deb's trajectory was a steady climb, but not all leadership journeys have to move that way. Michelle Gethers-Clark, CEO in a regional market for an international organization that funds nonprofits, spent the first part of her career in a global financial services firm. In the early days she worked her way up through the company. After earning her CPA, Michelle decided she wanted to lead people. She diversified her accounting and analytical skills to get more management experience. To do that, she knew she would have to leave the finance division of the company she was working for. So she approached her boss. "I said I appreciated what he'd done for me, but it was time for me to move on," Michelle told us. She asked for his support and endorsement as she weighed different opportunities. "At the time I was traveling a lot and I was single, and I wanted to have a family. I had an eye toward moving from finance to risk management."

DO YOU SHOW AGENCY?

Michelle and Deb are examples of women who demonstrate their agency. They had clarity and intention about their careers and sought opportunities that aligned with their career aspirations. They're great examples, but how do you practice your own brand of agency? What does effective agency look like? In *Standing at the Crossroads*, Marian Ruderman and Patty Ohlott describe eight ways to identify your brand of agency:

Clarity of direction. The work you did on identifying your intentions and core values in Chapter 1 is an important foundation for building your clarity of direction. How clear are you about your goals and desires? Are you clear about why you have chosen the goals you selected, or are you seeking to achieve just for achievement's sake? Women who have clarity of direction think about the long- and short-term implications of their decisions.

Planful action. Women who exercise agency don't sit around and wait to be called off the bench. They have a plan and consistently advocate for themselves to advance their long- and short-term goals.

Taking calculated risks. Do you push yourself out of your comfort zone, or do you wait until you feel 100 percent sure that you can do the job before you go for it? Women skilled at acting with agency take calculated risks. They have a growth mindset that allows them to overcome their fears and hesitation. They are neither overly optimistic nor pessimistic but have a deep sense of reality about what they are signing up for.

Self-awareness. Women with agency know themselves well— really well. They understand their values and have thought through their choices and trade-offs.

Adaptability to changing circumstances. A woman with agency understands that "shit happens." Sometimes you have to change your plans or take another route to get to where you want. When roadblocks arise, such women find another way. The operative word for such agency is *flexibility*. She's not thrown by obstacles or adversity because she's willing to be flexible and find alternate paths to her goal.

Resilience. Women with agency have deep reserves of confidence, believe in themselves, and rely on a strong inner core that allows them to thrive despite setbacks and challenges.

Learning. In CCL's Women's Leadership Experience course, we challenge women to talk about their most "glorious failures." Too often, women fear that failure makes them appear weak. But failure is necessary for growth. Are you crushed and cowed by failure, or do you see it as just one step closer to finding the answer? Are you learning from experience so you don't make the same mistakes twice? Women who effectively use agency are able to step back and realistically assess their mistakes, learn, and move forward without regret.

Letting go. Like the song in the popular Disney movie *Frozen*, women with agency realize that not everything is within their control, so they focus on the things they can control and don't sweat what they can't. Let it go. Just let it go.

AGENCY'S ROLE IN CAREER GOALS

All of the women we spoke to exhibited a high degree of agency when it came to managing their careers. We were curious about what men would say about women and career agency. Their view was that women were sometimes too passive in their approach to their careers, letting things happen to them rather than "taking charge" like their male counterparts often do. Overwhelmingly, these men didn't think it was because of any weakness or deficiency in the women they worked with but rather likely because of social and self-imposed constraints. So we asked for their perspective on what women could do to exert more agency. The advice they gave was the same as they gave to men. For example, Michael McAfee, CEO of a policy institute, had a no-nonsense perspective on the question:

> Figure out what trade-offs you want to make. When you are not in alignment you'll spend time chasing stuff. Lay out an arc in your career that makes sense to you. Can you create a storyboard of what you want to do in your career? Figure out the sectors you want to make your mark in. Have a plan. Lay this alongside what you value and the impact you want to make. Ask, what is my narrative? Most jobs aren't designed to give us what we want. . . . You have to go out and get what you want!

Michael's challenge is profound. What is your narrative? What is your unique contribution? Develop your unique point of view and go get what you want! We love this perspective. If you have done the work to identify your values and clarify your intentions as explained in Chapter 1, his words probably hit home for you. If this isn't clear for you, we urge you to go back to Chapter 1 and work through the Values Explorer exercise.

WHAT'S GETTING IN THE WAY OF YOUR AGENCY?

You may have the best intentions but still struggle to act with agency. What gets in your way? In our experience, women may encounter several challenges:

Discomfort with Authority

Most of the leaders we spoke to could distinctly remember the moment when they rose to a position of authority where they were "the decider." Achieving that first leadership role—the place where the buck stops with you—can be exhilarating and terrifying. Women with agency are comfortable with authority and with power. It can be hard for some women to reach that level of comfort because they are often taught from a young age to defer to authority, and they are often put in positions that play supporting roles to authority figures.

From CCL's point of view, developing leadership is an iterative process.[3] No one wakes up one morning suddenly feeling confident and secure about being the leader. Confidence comes from being tested, from failure and success, and from trying out new approaches in a supportive environment. This is why it's important to take on challenging assignments that allow you to try out new behaviors in low-risk environments and get feedback from trusted mentors and sponsors.

Deb, the president of the craft and novelty company we mentioned earlier, puts it this way: "It takes a while to learn how to act like an executive. Most women are not used to acting like executives. It wasn't until later in my career that I got comfortable with wearing the mantle of the presidency. There is a certain confidence that comes over time. Women are more used to being in a supportive function, as I was in the earlier days of my career. So it took a while to adjust—instead of advising, you are now deciding; instead of suggesting, you are now leading. It is a very different orientation, one that takes some getting used to. In my case, there was one other woman on the executive team who was a good role model for me, along with a male executive who actively mentored me when I first assumed the role as president of a large division. It made the transition a lot easier and faster."

Leslie Joyce's story dramatically illustrates those first frantic moments of acting confident when you take on your first leadership role. She had been hired at the age of 31 by a small firm as the VP of HR. "I didn't know shit about running HR! I was an industrial/organizational psychologist!" she says. Well, she found out what it takes to lead pretty fast when her company experienced a bomb threat less than 12 months after a disgruntled employee had made threats to the prior VP of HR. "Here I was, trying to run from floor to floor, trying to direct people and calm them down, assuring them they were safe, and I'm thinking, 'Why do they believe me? I'm just a kid! What the hell do I know?' That's when I got the first message about being young and female and in a leadership position. There are requirements of confidence and poise—executive presence. Most of the company's other leaders were older than me, and all were men. That was when I realized I needed to act much older than I actually was to be taken seriously."

To explore your own perspective on authority and power, grab your journal and write down your responses to these questions:

- How comfortable am I with taking authority and having power?

- How can I use my authority and power in ways that help me be my own agent?

- If I'm not comfortable with taking power and authority, what is getting in my way?

- How can I push myself through that discomfort?

- Whom can I enlist to support me as I build my comfort level?

Dysfunctional Work Environments

We know from our coaching work that people often endure dysfunctional work environments, from toxic bosses to unhealthy work cultures. These forces exert negative pressure on leaders and can cause women to doubt themselves and become hesitant—sometimes to the point of derailing their careers.

Jabu Dayton, whom we will revisit in Chapter 5, learned about hurtful environments in the early days of her HR consulting business in the competitive world of Silicon Valley start-ups. In more than a few of those companies, HR did not exist and wasn't appreciated by the founders. Jabu witnessed behavior she knew would never be tolerated at more established corporations and was aware that these behaviors put these businesses at risk for lawsuits. But learning about toxic work environments wasn't the only or the most profound lesson Jabu learned from her experiences.

"When I got in there [coming into a particular start-up], I still had my corporate hat on and saw things that just made no sense. I know I got on the founders' nerves because there is a right and a wrong way to do HR," Jabu says. "I was the oldest person at the start-up. None of the staff was over 30. Because of a previous bad corporate experience, I didn't want to be in a position of power. So I stepped away from the table and didn't push things I knew needed changing. That was a mess-up of immense proportions because now I didn't have a seat at the table. Now when I coach women and men of color, I always tell them *when you give away power, you won't get it back."*

As painful as these experiences were in the early days of her business, Jabu gained valuable insight into her own agency. Now she accepts clients based on stringent requirements, confirming that they share her values and that she aligns with the founders' leadership philosophy. Jabu now exercises agency about her career and about the kind of client experience she wants to have.

Not all lessons in agency require that you leave a toxic environment behind. Mary Beth Bardin, an entrepreneur and retired chief communications offer, decided to stick it out despite initially not being happy with her boss or the culture. She thought she needed a change in career and saw a counselor and took several assessments to discover what kind of job was the best use of her talents. Guess what? It was the job she already had. Mary Beth had a choice to make.

That was when she figured out that it wasn't her job so much as the environment that was making her miserable. "I adjusted my attitude," she says. "I made it all about the work. I will focus on creating the best work I can. I will tune out the environment." Mary Beth's boss wasn't a particularly good manager, and the company's culture was changing significantly. "I decided to stick it out because I liked the people I was working with. We started to produce really good work product and started to get recognition. I got promoted. My boss eventually left," she says. What did Mary Beth's agency—visible in the choice she made and in the work she did—teach her? "I tell people to find a good company and stay there if you can," she says.

Sometimes, you need agency to create the type of environment in which you and others can thrive. In Chapter 1 we met Susana Marin, general manager of a luxury hotel in Spain: "In my early years I worked as a trainee in two five-star hotels in the city during the Olympics. Although both were good work experiences, unfortunately, I did not have very good leadership models in either of the hotels. I had an early shift in one hotel and a late shift in the second one. In between, I had the chance to spend some time in Plaza Catalunya (the main city square), where many tourists and visitors passed by. By observing people I saw that there were three types of locals. One type of local would just pass by and ignore a family who appeared lost. The second type would slow down. If they were asked for help, they would stop and help. But if they were not asked, they would pass by. The third type would stop and offer help. No matter the language barrier or the possibility of not knowing the answer, they had this urge to stop. I shared the same feeling. I selfishly needed to help, to feel like an ambassador of my city, and to get instant gratification when influencing others. This part of the day was the most inspiring for me in my pursuit to be part of a company that would promote this service environment and to learn to be the leader of this type of company culture for others."

Where are you in terms of acting with agency? Answer the following questions in your journal.

- If your current work environment is keeping you from acting with agency, what can you do to be your own agent in spite of it?

- Who else can you enlist to change the work environment?

Lack of Self-Clarity

The difference between self-awareness and self-clarity is subtle but profound.[4] Self-awareness is about understanding your strengths and weaknesses, and self-clarity is about having a deep sense of purpose, knowing who you are and your place in the world. Women with self-clarity understand their choices and trade-offs. They deeply understand their preferences and align their actions to meet those preferences. They have drawn their road map and understand the terrain they must navigate to reach their goal. They have done the kind of work that you began in Chapter 1. Key to self-clarity is a realistic view of the world and an avoidance of magical thinking. Such women have a realistic assessment of the world that is neither overly pessimistic nor too optimistic. Sometimes self-clarity comes from periods of reflection and learning. At other times is it thrust upon you.

As a young woman, Christine Malcolm, a board director and retired hospital administrator, dreamed of becoming a doctor. She studied biology in college with plans of going to medical school after graduation. Before medical school, while still in her twenties, she married and took a job as an administrative intern in her native Minnesota. Suddenly, a catastrophic illness altered her life plans.

"I got a ruptured appendix and spleen, developed gangrene, went to the hospital in May, and came out in September," Christine recalls. "I was in a coma for 21 days. I had brain damage and was on the edge of dying for a long time. In the hospital, I had a lot of time to observe the hospital staff and realized I didn't want to be a doctor. Doctors saw people every 15 minutes. People came in, left, and then came back sicker. I didn't want to do that. I wanted to build things and help to create sustainable change. So I went to business school at the University of Chicago to become a hospital administrator. I never questioned my decision."

Christine's powerful self-clarity came from her near-death experience. She gained a realistic view of the physician's life and realized it wasn't a life she wanted for herself. We're happy to tell you that you don't have to endure a life-threatening illness to gain self-clarity. But why should you care about whether you have self-clarity? There are many reasons, but it all boils down to this: Self-clarity will help you deal with the daily challenges of life. You'll be better able to handle the obstacles that will inevitably come your way. Self-clarity enables you to draw upon your self-knowledge, the convictions of your values, purpose, and intentions. When you are clear about who you are and why, you can see that obstacles are temporary. In your personal and professional life, you will encounter moments filled with ambiguity. Your sense of self-clarity can serve as your North Star when all else seems fuzzy and uncertain.

If you're uncertain about how to reach your own self-clarity, go back to your responses to the values exploration in Chapter 1. A solid understanding of your intent and purpose, and the will to live in a way that aligns with them, lays the foundation for self-clarity.

Outdated Mental Models

The novelist Anaïs Nin once wrote, "We don't see things as they are; we see things as we are."[5] Nin was pointing to the idea of mental models, a psychological term for deeply ingrained assumptions, generalizations, and even images that influence how we understand the world and how we take action in response to it. Sometimes we work with outdated mental models. They filter what we pay attention to, guide our interpretations of our experiences, and inform our actions. Our mental models can hold us back from opportunities that we should take because they prevent us from seeing what is possible. When we carry outdated mental models, we can sometimes make choices that aren't in alignment with or run counter to our current values and expressed intentions.

Take Lina Papadopoulos (a pseudonym), for example, who lives and works in Alaska. An electrical engineer and director of operations at an oil company, Lina is the lone woman in her division. She loves her job and also loves being a mother to four kids (and twins on the way!) and an active member of her community. When we met she was working hard to earn a promotion that would enable her to transfer to the company's Houston headquarters and put her closer to her goal of becoming a vice president of operations. If she could reach that goal, she'd be one of the first women in that role in the company's history. At the time of our meeting she was pregnant with twins, caring for the four young children she had at home, working 70 hours a week, traveling sometimes several times a month, and volunteering on several local community boards.

No surprise, Lina was exhausted. Her doctor warned her that a twin pregnancy would likely lead to bed rest if she didn't slow down. It's not what she wanted to hear. She was goal oriented. The youngest in a large Greek family, she was the first to go to college. She'd grown up poor, and financial stability was a core value for her. She was consumed with work and feared that if she slowed down, she'd miss a crucial career opportunity. She rarely took vacation time. And when we asked her about her maternity leave plans, she admitted she hadn't thought much about it.

An ultimatum from her doctor challenged Lina to review her schedule. Did she really need to serve on so many community boards? What was she gaining from taking so few days off work? During coaching sessions, we challenged her to examine the impact her choices had on her family and her physical health. Lina admitted it was hard for her to slow down. She wanted to spend more time with her family and savor the success she had worked so hard for but never had time to enjoy. Her husband was handling most of the work on the home front. Her young children rarely saw her during the week, and the little time she did have with them felt rushed and unsatisfying. She felt she was letting her husband and her family down. While she was financially well off, her fear of falling into poverty drove her to work long hours.

Lina's outdated mental model held her in its grip. She grew up in poverty and still financially supported many of her siblings. She sat on many boards because she valued community involvement but also feared that a lack of visibility would reduce her career opportunities. She admitted that, as the youngest of eight children, she had always felt invisible and craved recognition that made her feel validated. As a result of her mental models, she never felt she could truly savor her success.

After understanding the mental models that were operating in her life, Lina made some tough decisions. She stepped away from most of her community engagements so she could preserve her health and spend more time with her family. She found a senior-level sponsor in the company who agreed to advise her on her career path at the company going forward. Most important, she gave herself permission to slow down and take time for herself so she could appreciate her family and all that she had achieved thus far in her life, something she hadn't been able to do previously.

Mental models aren't necessarily negative. In some situations they might limit your actions based on your interpretations of a situation. But in others they can provoke you to go further and achieve more than you might have expected. My (Portia's) own example shows how that works.

I grew up the oldest of three children in a middle-class black family in the United States. My family lived in predominately white neighborhoods and was often the only black family around. We called ourselves "The Williams Five." School was no different. I was frequently the only black student in my advanced classes. I was in the second generation of my family to attend college. My parents emphasized the importance of education and achievement. When I was in high school, they warned me about going to parties where there was alcohol and underlined that I might be the only black person there: "You will be noticeable wherever you go. If there is only one face they remember, it will be yours. Don't forget that."

My parents told me that I had to be better than most other students because schools and communities often set low expectations for black kids. As a result, I came to believe that in order to be accepted in predominately white environments, I needed to be twice as good as my white counterparts—especially at work where I might be judged as an "affirmative action hire." In my career, much as in my early academic life, I was frequently one of the only black executives wherever I worked. While I rarely experienced overt racism, I often felt I had to prove my competence over and over, especially when I began a new job where I didn't have a track record. I could imagine my white coworkers wondering, "How did she get this job? Does she really know what she's doing?" My mother's words were never far from my mind: "Remember, no matter what, you are the one who stands out. You must be better."

My mental model of achievement, shaped in part by being the only black person in many of the environments I lived and worked in, deeply affected my approach to my work and how I lived my life. Under its influence, I achieved great success.

OWN YOUR POWER OF AGENCY

Owning your power by asserting your sense of agency is the ultimate path to living the life you want and having the career you most desire. When what you want seems out of reach or when setbacks occur (and they will happen), your sense of agency will fuel your energy and focus. When you've clarified your most important values and understand your intentions, you can wake up each morning knowing you have the inner drive and motivation to succeed.

To measure where you are in terms of your own agency and the power you can derive from it, follow this exercise:

Review the following questions and circle the best answer using this scale:

1 = strongly agree
2 = agree
3 = neutral
4 = disagree
5 = strongly disagree

1. When opportunities come that fit my qualifications, I can advocate for myself.

    1   2   3   4   5

2. I have clarity about what is important to me, and don't hesitate to go after what I want.

    1   2   3   4   5

3. I am comfortable with being in roles of authority and using power to accomplish my goals.

    1   2   3   4   5

4. I take calculated risks to help me achieve my goals.

    1   2   3   4   5

5. I'm not afraid to fail and view failure as a critical component of success.

    1   2   3   4   5

6. I am resilient and am not deterred by challenges or setbacks.

    1   2   3   4   5

7. I am able to say no to things that don't align with my intentions, values, or priorities.

    1   2   3   4   5

8. I have a strong sense of self-clarity and use that on a daily basis to prioritize my actions.

    1   2   3   4   5

9. I am able to learn from my experiences so that I can improve my decisions and actions in the future.

    1   2   3   4   5

10. I am able to flex and adapt to changing circumstances so that my actions better fit the reality of the moment.

    1   2   3   4   5

If you answered mostly 1s or 2s, you are comfortable acting with agency. If you answered mostly 4s and 5s, you may need to work on reaching that level of comfort. If acting with agency is challenging for you or you would just like to get better at it, consider the following questions. Use your journal to capture the thoughts and feelings that the questions spark in you.

- What's in it for me if I learn to act with more agency?

- Conversely, what do I lose if I don't act with agency?

- What is one step I can take tomorrow to act with agency?

- What resources can I tap to help me be more accountable so that I can act with more agency?

- Which of the eight ways to demonstrate agency described in this chapter am I best at?

- Which of the eight ways to demonstrate agency do I need to improve? (If I've identified more than two or three, how can I prioritize what I might work on first?)

- Which of the obstacles to agency do I experience, and how can I resolve them?

- What mental models do I carry that influence my views on agency?

- Do my mental models keep me from acting with full agency? (Am I more often passive than assertive?)

- Do my mental models help me understand why I make the decisions I do?

- Reflecting on my mental models, I am surprised by _____.

- What aspect(s) of my mental models no longer serves me? Why not?

- What aspect(s) of my mental models do I want to hold on to? Why?

Success Your Way

Success for me means being secure financially, spiritually, and emotionally and having a level of satisfaction in all of those things.

—Chaton Turner, Assistant Counsel,
University of Pittsburgh Medical Center

In this chapter, you will learn:

- How to come up with your own definition of success that aligns with your values and intentions
- Why it may be time to reinvent your career
- Why a glorious failure can be a springboard to opportunity

When I (Portia) was in my twenties, I met Linda Taylor, a prominent Kansas City attorney. Linda had been one of the few women partners in a major law firm anywhere in the United States. She had recently left that firm to start her own business. Over lunch one day, I asked Linda why she left such a lucrative and prominent position to start her own business. What Linda shared next stuck with me: "You can keep climbing and striving for that next position. But when you get there, suddenly you realize there is no 'there' there. It's all an illusion."

Rising to prominence at one of the country's largest and most prominent law firms was not as fulfilling as Linda had hoped or expected. After much soul-searching, she took a gamble to start a temporary services firm supporting the legal profession—something virtually unheard of at the time but that would ultimately pay off both financially and professionally. Linda's caution to me was not to define success simply by a title or compensation. Those things are superficial to understanding what truly feeds one's soul and sense of purpose. It was only after leaving the relative safety of a law firm and striking out on her own that Linda truly felt she was fulfilling her calling.

FIND YOUR VIEW OF SUCCESS

As we interviewed executives around the world, Linda's words continued to resonate for us. More than that, they were echoed by the leaders to whom we spoke. We heard over and over that the outward trappings of success—salary, title, and recognition—are rarely enough. These executives didn't think about success in material terms, but crafted their own definitions of success, which they worked toward in their daily lives.

Heather Banks, chief human resources officer of a mid-Atlantic manufacturing company, says that, for her, success is not defined by material things. "It's about what impact do I have in the world. I try to live my life and ask, 'Is the story I'm living the one I want to be writing? Would I be happy to have someone tell my story and be proud of it? To know I have made a positive impact on all of the people I am holding space for? Am I raising my children to be empathic people, to use their knowledge for the greater good?' That is the story that I want to be telling."

To a person, the executives we spoke with defined success as fulfilling their sense of purpose and their ability to have an impact on the people and issues they cared about. Their definitions of success universally included having deep meaningful relationships and having the time to invest in those relationships.

TAKE TIME TO REFLECT

What does success mean for you? Go back and look at the values you identified in Chapter 1. Think about the intentions you set. And from Chapter 2, think about how the mental models you hold influence your definition of success. As we described earlier, mental models are ingrained assumptions, generalizations, and even images that influence how we understand the world and how we take action.

To see how mental models affect definitions of success, consider that several executives we spoke with grew up in working-class families in which they were the first in their family to go to college. They worked to put themselves through school. For many of these executives, their mental models focused on financial security and the ability to retire before age 50 as a benchmark for success. Early in their careers they established specific career and salary targets each year that would enable them to achieve that goal. That's a perfectly fine approach as long as it aligns with your values, intentions, and sense of purpose. But underline this: Your definition of success shouldn't be someone else's. It's yours alone. The journey you are on is deeply personal, and it's tempting to let others define what you should or shouldn't aspire to. That's the hidden power of mental models: they can influence you to accept someone else's measure of success without you being fully aware that you're under their influence.

Susi Takeuchi is a chief human resources officer of a university hospital system. Relying on her own version of success seems like the only way to feel real, fulfilled, and energized. "I feel that most people have a deep need to recognize their full potential," she says. "Had I listened to the advice of 'Just put your head down and be happy,' I would still be unfulfilled." Susi advises career women not to cheat themselves out of opportunities, even when the shadow of impostor syndrome (see Chapter 5) looms. "Sometimes I would feel like this job is over my head," she says. "But you have to be a little scared. If you feel like the job is a piece of cake, you aren't challenging yourself." Susi summed up her markers of success: to be intellectually challenged, to feel like she was contributing to her organization, and to help others develop and grow. She has carried those measures throughout her career.

TAKE YOUR MEASURE

Here is a short exercise for practicing the reflection and determination you need to define your own success measures. You'll need your journal handy to reflect and write. First, ask yourself, "What does success mean for me?" Don't hurry. Take some time to think deeply about what success looks and feels like for you. Be specific in your description: What are you doing when you are most successful? What are you feeling? No doubt you will find that your definition of success includes not only career aspects but also touches your personal life—reflect on those connections as well. Use your journal to jot down your thoughts and feelings and to work through your reflections.

YOU DON'T NEED A DETAILED MAP, BUT YOU DO NEED A PATH

When we asked executives to reflect on their careers, we were surprised to learn that rarely did they have a set career plan that they followed; rather, they had a set of deeply held values and beliefs that guided their career and life decisions. The fact that they became successful (some wildly so) was almost tangential to their ability to live life according to a set of self-identified values and intentions.

That sounds counterintuitive, right? After all, we were talking to successful career women and men. Surely they plotted and planned their way to career success. Surely they had mapped every move. We found out that it was usually the opposite. A few of the executives to whom we spoke did say they aspired to a specific title, position, or even compensation. But what we heard most frequently was something like, "I wanted to get to a position where I could learn, have the most impact, and add the most value with my skill set." These are smart, ambitious, high-achieving people. That general idea often raised them to the most senior positions in their organizations. We also noticed some commonality among the women we spoke to. They had clearly defined values and priorities that guided their decisions about their career and life choices.

Do any of these themes resonate for you?

- They were consistent in living their values and priorities but flexible in how they executed these in their daily lives. When something didn't work or there was a better option, they didn't hesitate to make a change.

- They understood their choices and trade-offs for career and life and proactively managed those choices and trade-offs to optimize their decisions.

- They had strong mentors and sponsors who could provide crucial guidance at key moments in their lives.

- They were prepared to reinvent their careers when necessary to better align with their values, concept of themselves, and current priorities.

- They didn't overpersonalize failure and understood it was an opportunity to learn and grow rather than a reflection of a personal deficit.

Steve Reinemund, board member and retired CEO, shares this advice: "Have a life purpose and a life vision and measure yourself against that. I grew up with a single mom because my father passed away when I was young. She stressed the importance of having a purpose. Mom is the hero of my life. With her in mind, I set a life purpose to have a balance between faith, family, and work in a way that reflected my priorities." Sounds good to us.

Wait, Madonna Is a Teacher Now?

Look at those last two bullet points: reinvention and failure. Now think about how Madonna, who burst onto the eighties scene as a young club kid to become a pop superstar to Gen X, shocked the pop music world with her performance of "Like a Virgin" at the MTV Video Music Awards in 1984, and created a visual lexicon that is still being imitated today. She continuously evolves her look and her sound, not simply to remain relevant but to set the pace for legions of entertainers many years her junior. Over the years she has defied an industry that is particularly harsh toward aging female entertainers.

Now entering her sixties, Madonna still challenges conventions about how a woman of a certain age should act or look. We love her for that. In response to a question about her continuous reinvention, she was quoted as saying, "Life and love inspire me. I think reinventing yourself is vital to your survival as an artist and a human being. I know it's cliché to say about me at this point, but it's true. My curiosity definitely is the driving force in my life and career. When you stop learning, engaging, and growing, you're dead."

There's only one Madonna, but you can take a page from her book and also evolve how you think about yourself, your career, and your life, regardless of what others may think. In a perfect world, we'd figure out our passions and purpose and set out on a perfectly aligned career to match. But get real. Most of us, at some point, will change jobs and maybe even careers multiple times. According to the National Bureau of Labor Statistics, adults will hold an average of 11 jobs over their working lifetime.[1] If you are in the millennial generation, you will probably have four jobs your first decade after college or by the time you turn 32.[2] A whole lot of change going on—and that's not a bad thing because as you change and evolve, your career aspirations will change along with you.

LEAP AND THE NET WILL APPEAR

It sounds like bad advice given to an acrobat, but actually it's a message of faith. Faith in yourself, your values, intent, and purpose. Faith in the path you're following because it follows those measures. It's the message Kalyn Johnson Chandler was given by a close friend. She is now a successful entrepreneur of an online company that sells cool stationery, desk accessories, and travel/coffee mugs. She has branded herself as a tastemaker and has become a social media star, which makes her backstory all the more compelling. But that wasn't where she had thought she'd end up. You see, Kalyn calls herself a recovering corporate attorney.

Kalyn never planned to have a law career but (like many who go into law) was lured by the intellectual stimulation and hefty paycheck that would help her pay off her school loans. Ten years into her career at a major New York law firm, she was still intellectually stimulated, but the stress and glass ceiling were getting to her. Working even harder to get onto the partner track held no appeal at all. What was next? A mistake that almost killed her law career answered that question for her.

During a much-needed vacation to Florida, Kalyn was hit by a dramatic situation at her law firm caused by an error she had made. "I checked my BlackBerry when I landed in Miami and was faced with a barrage of e-mails," she remembers. "I learned I had made a mistake before I left for vacation and it had the potential to derail an important deal. I was supposed to be on vacation, so I hadn't brought my laptop with me. So I spent the weekend using the computer and services at Kinko's. When [now husband] Todd showed up, I burst into tears. 'This isn't you,' he said."

Her disastrous weekend was Kalyn's turning point. She knew she had to make a change. But to what? She took a step back and asked herself, "Do I really want to be practicing law?" She had interviewed for a number of opportunities with other law firms, but none of them really felt right. "I was deathly afraid of not practicing law because it was 'safe,'" Kalyn says. "But, once I walked away from that last opportunity, I knew I didn't really want to practice law anymore." A conversation with a dear friend challenged her thinking. Her friend's advice? *"Leap and the net will appear."* And from another friend? *"If you don't do it, you'll never know."*

Kalyn credits the combination of those two conversations with making her comfortable enough to walk away from practicing law. Those conversations not only prodded her to look elsewhere for meaningful success, but they helped her feel more secure leaving a field she was comfortable in. "I took the leap and left on May 7, 2011," she says. "I took a couple of months and did nothing. I visited friends and family, read books, shredded papers, and really decompressed."

As her recovery progressed, Kalyn realized that her love of fashion might offer an answer to the "what next?" question. She frequently helped her colleagues and friends style their wardrobes. Was that her net? She launched her styling business with a focus on professional women, leveraging her law firm and corporate contacts. She learned that while she enjoyed shopping for clients, lugging bags of clothing around Manhattan, combined with her clients' reluctance to pay her adequately for her time, wasn't going to cut it. Maybe it wasn't her net. Then came the Great Recession, and her clients lost the discretionary income they had spent on clothes. Her net had been cut.

It was while she was planning her wedding that Kalyn had her eureka moment. While working with a graphic designer on her wedding stationery, it hit her to launch her own stationery company, Effie's Paper :: Stationery&Whatnot, named after her grandmother who loved stationery and had worked for a greeting card company throughout Kalyn's childhood.

Oh, but That's Not Going to Work

If you're thinking, "Well, that's fine for Kalyn, but I can't afford to leave my job without another job," consider Susan Tardanico's situation. Susan spent years as a chief communications officer for a global industrial manufacturing company. As the company and leadership changed, she became more aware that the match between her values, her vision for her life, and the company to which she dedicated countless hours were beginning to misalign. There was never enough time to do the mission critical things that were required of her. Her role as a corporate officer was a 24/7 commitment, and it was taking a toll on her personal life. As she realized she was off track from her personal view of success, she also realized she would have to leave corporate life.

"I wanted to reclaim my own life and have more freedom, flexibility, and a greater sense of control," Susan says. "I started to feel like the values of the organization weren't consistent with my own."

"I was burnt out and had been on a sprint for eight years," Susan recalls. "It was 24/7 and all-consuming. I wanted to be able to breathe again and have more impact. When you are part of a big corporate machine, managing politics is a major focus. You are just trying to prevent things from happening. I wanted to get closer to my craft versus being in management—I knew several years before I left that I wanted to leave."

Since she knew she wanted to leave her job, Susan became very strategic about saving money and spent time thinking about what her first and second year outside of corporate life might look like. She even thought about how much time she'd give herself to succeed or fail because she was walking away from a substantial corporate salary. Susan spent a few years getting herself ready to make her move, and then she took that leap, ultimately launching a successful leadership and coaching consulting practice.

What lessons can we learn from Kalyn and Susan about career reinvention? Here are a few we learned from them and our coaching clients:

- **Recognize the signs when your current job is no longer meeting your needs.** Often the job we most wanted when we initially pursued it is no longer a fit. Companies and leadership change all the time. We evolve, too, and as we get to know ourselves, what we value and need changes. Often the company we initially went to work for no longer aligns with our values. Susan discovered this and made a plan to pursue more meaningful work that was aligned with who she was. Don't be afraid to say, "This is no longer working for me." It doesn't mean failure. It means you are growing! Embrace the opportunity you've been presented!

- **Make time to explore outside interests.** Read, take classes, really explore the interests you have that perhaps you've put aside because of other priorities. Use this exploration to lay the foundation for a potential new career or simply a passion you want to engage in regularly. If you need to stay in your current role, at least give yourself space to imagine that next step. Kalyn was doing nothing related to her paying job when she had the idea to start a stationery company—she was working on her wedding invitations. So take walks, doodle, meditate, or do whatever gives your brain the mental space to allow new ideas to bloom. Give yourself enough room to discover your next success.

- **Lay the groundwork for your next move.** Most of us can't just pull the plug on our current job and live without an income indefinitely. Susan created a plan that included determining how much money she would need to live her current lifestyle without a corporate salary and began saving money. She also determined how much time she'd give herself to succeed in her new endeavor. Thinking through these steps allowed her flexibility and the ability to "de-risk" aspects of her next move so she could confidently quit her job when it was time.

- **Start a side hustle.** Rather than quit your job outright, explore your interests as a volunteer or consultant. See where these experiences lead you. Can your explorations become your jumping-off place?

- **Gather a group of advisors.** Let's face it, career change can be downright terrifying. Don't go it alone. Kalyn found a group of like-minded women who were striking out on their own to build their own businesses. One of them became an accountability partner for her, propping her up when she became discouraged and kicking her in the backside when her motivation flagged and she wasn't meeting her goals. Find a group of friends, mentors, or sponsors who can be both supportive and challenging as you plot your next move. Chapter 4 will help you find your group.

- **Be prepared to adapt and iterate during your reinvention.** Like Kalyn, your first postcareer move may not be where you finally land, but it will provide you information about what really makes your heart leap.

You may be ready to reinvent your career if any of these are true for you:

- You feel like there is a misalignment between your organization's values and your own.

- You no longer feel energy or passion for what you do.

- You feel you are not having an impact, and you can make more of a difference elsewhere.

- You are in a toxic or dysfunctional environment that drains your energy.

- You feel like you've accomplished all you planned in your current role and don't see opportunities for yourself there.

- You often daydream of pursuing outside interests.

If you are having any of these thoughts, consider reimagining your career where you are or start planning a move that gets you closer to a career that is more in line with your vision. Go for it!

GLORIOUS FAILURE

Reinvention and success come with failure. Every executive we spoke to experienced failure on some level. Failure can be tricky for overachievers who are used to creating plans, grinding out the work, and then winning. Failure may set some leaders back, but the executives we talked to were tenacious, and they kept going until they reached their goals despite obstacles.

Carol Dweck says that an important part of that ability to go on in the face of failure is a *growth mindset*.[3] Our mindsets, says Dweck, can be characterized as *fixed* or *growth*. People with a fixed mindset tend to believe that their basic qualities, like their talent or intelligence, are fairly fixed traits. They focus on demonstrating their capabilities rather than developing them. They want to achieve and win. High performance is critical for them to feel successful. On the other hand, people with a growth mindset believe that they can develop their abilities and improve them, so they put their efforts into practice, hard work, failing and trying again, and learning. In Dweck's experience, and in what we heard from the women and men we interviewed, people who define themselves as successful exercise a growth mindset.

When you stretch yourself, you encounter failure. This is a 100 percent certainty. It might be a small setback. It might knock you to the floor. But if you're not failing, you aren't experimenting enough. A colleague who works in Silicon Valley told us about sessions her company hosts where entrepreneurs get together and talk about their biggest failures (imagine!) and what they've learned. We love that. It's important to bust the myth that successful people don't fail. If you spend any time on social media, you might not think that's the case, right? We live in a hypercurated world where people carefully shape the images they present. People post about their great new jobs, their fabulous vacations, the amazing meals they've eaten, and their brilliant children. It's all about success that seems to have happened overnight. How often do your read about someone's failure? You don't. But we need failure because failure gives us data we didn't previously have. And we can use that knowledge to refine our decisions and clarify our vision. Failure is a necessary part of becoming the best version of ourselves.

Some of CCL's foundational research focuses on understanding the types of experiences that leaders believe have led to the greatest lessons learned.[4] Failures are one of the types of "hardship" experiences from which leaders learn—experiences such as making business mistakes, pulling out of a career rut or a lousy job, and dealing with problem employees. Some of the lessons learned from these types of hardships include learning what is really important in terms of one's personal or professional life; where one's strengths or weaknesses lie and how they point to the types of jobs and careers that would be a good fit; and how to be in charge of one's own career and formulate strategies to keep moving toward a vision of success.

In CCL's women's leadership program, the Women's Leadership Experience, we ask women to think about their most glorious failure and talk about it with their peers. Why do we do this? Over the course of the program, we challenge women to experiment with new behaviors and ways of working that take them out of their comfort zone. Some of these experiments in new ways of being will be successful, while others will fall flat. And that's OK! What is most important is what's been learned.

In our research and conversations, we've observed that women and men experience failure differently. While women see failure as the result of a personal shortcoming, men often depersonalize it and view it as something that was beyond their control and not necessarily a personal reflection on their ability.

Steve, the board member and retired CEO, shared an anecdote from his early days as a young restaurant executive.

Steve thought his plan for pizza delivery for Pizza Hut was a sure thing, but it turned into what he calls his "biggest personal failure." In the mideighties he was running Pizza Hut when it was just entering the pizza delivery business. He put together a proposal that the board funded. The plan fell flat. Within months Pizza Hut began losing $1 million a month on a $52 million annual expected profit. He says, "To this day, I don't know why I wasn't fired. But I went back to my boss after a few months and said, 'This isn't working.' He said, 'I know. What are you going to do to fix it?'" Steve's boss said the vision of the plan was right, but the execution was wrong.

Steve developed another proposal, and although it took two and a half years, his idea eventually led to success. "That experience through that two and half years from failure to success was the most important two and a half years of my career. What I learned, and what others saw in me, was how I dealt with failure."

From his leadership role, Steve watches how people deal with and overcome failures, and his observations guide his selection to major promotions. "Life is not all successes because not all of life is success," Steve says. "I see people take jobs where they don't want risk. These people fail at the top because they haven't had to deal with the reality of failure. Every day you will have successes and failures. It is how you deal with it that matters."

The Tibetan Buddhist nun Pema Chodron encourages us to "fail, fail again, fail better."[5] Often, as women, when we experience failure, we internalize it, thinking, "I'm a failure" rather than "This thing I really cared about didn't work out. Why?" Chodron challenges us to be curious about failure and not to ignore the emotions such as grief, rage, and befuddlement that accompany it. Failure often brings an opportunity to step back and look at the big picture. In your career, failure can be your springboard forward.

SET A HIGH BAR

Ironically, many people we interviewed gave us the sense that they had not yet been, and may never be, successful. What?! Women and men who have made it to the top levels in their organizations don't see themselves as successful? What's that about? It's because they have set their sights on success being something beyond a job or a career. They look at success as the legacy they are leaving, the contribution they are making to the world, the impact they are having on others' lives.

YOUR WAY TO SUCCESS

A little earlier we asked you to reflect in your journal about what success means to you. Did you define success as happening in your current job? Or did you define it from a perspective of success in life? If you lived a successful life, what would people say about you once you were gone?

Once you have that big picture in your mind, sketch out your journey from where you are now to where you would be then. Have fun with it—draw a straight line or a very winding path—whatever works for you!

Do you see any particular experiences you think you need to have along your journey? If yes, and if you have specific thoughts about how to gain those experiences, put them on your journey map wherever it feels right to you.

If you were to take a leap right now, what would it be? Add some thoughts to your journey map about the type of leap you would take. Does it mean leaving your current job? Or can you take a leap by stepping out of your comfort zone and trying something new while you're still in your current job?

There is no one definition of success and how to get there. It's all about what works for you. You don't need a plan, but you do need a path to pursue your vision of success. How you get there is totally up to you. But how will you know you are there? This will depend on your values (yes, we are going to keep returning to these throughout the book), your intentions, your unique contribution. Are you realizing those? Are you fulfilling your deepest intentions? Are you making a contribution? Is the story you are writing one that you would like others to tell? If so, congratulations, you are on your way!

You can be successful, no matter how winding your journey is and how many times you feel like you're taking a step backward. If you are open to redefining success throughout your career and your life, as long as you feel you are headed in the right direction, you will get there!

QUESTIONS FOR REFLECTION

Open your journal and answer these questions:

- What is my most glorious failure?

- How did I feel in the moment of that failure?

- What did that experience teach me that I can carry forward as I step out of my comfort zone to achieve my vision for my life?

- Am I ready to reinvent my career?

- Should I change jobs or make adjustments to the one I have?

Write on these questions until you have filled up at least two pages in your journal. Don't worry about the quality of your writing. Don't edit yourself. Now use this last question to think about your next steps:

- What are one or two actions I can take right now to begin to have a career that is more aligned with my authentic self?

CHAPTER

Build Your Network of Champions

*I could not have done it without mentors. The best
mentors I ever had told me what was difficult to
hear. They told me the brutal truth. To their credit
they were honest, and to my credit I could bear it.*

—Mary Beth Bardin, former Chief
Communications Officer, Verizon

In this chapter, you will learn:

- The importance of developing a network who can help you
  develop and gain access to new opportunities and new
  connections
- The ways that mentors and sponsors can help you
- How to map your professional network

Can we agree on something right away? None of us, of any gender, succeed on our own. In work, in life, in relationships—nowhere. Can you imagine a world where you always live, work, eat, exercise, and relax all by yourself? Of course not! By nature, human beings are connected to other people. Some of us more than others, sure, but it's the rare individual who goes through life with absolutely no contact, relationship, reliance, or influence from others—either intentional or not. Other people will play a role in our success and our failure.

So when it comes to your leadership success, there has been someone (maybe multiple someones) who has influenced you in some way along your journey. Someone may have provided advice, acted as a role model, been a horrible boss or peer, shown you the ropes when you took a new job, or introduced you to the person who offered you your next professional role. The people around us—our network—have the ability either to support us or to hinder our growth into the leaders we're meant to be.

These people have many different names and titles. In this chapter, we call them *mentors*, *sponsors*, and *members* of our networks. Each of these roles is critical for people who want to grow in their leadership capability, and there are differences among them that are important to understand. Yet all of them demonstrate what CCL has learned from its research on how leaders learn through other people. In the groundbreaking Lessons of Experience research,[1] often called the 70-20-10 research, Morgan McCall, Mike Lombardo, and Ann Morrison identified that leaders gain about 20 percent of their leadership learning experiences through relationships with other people.

REALITY CHECK

Before we dive into those specific developmental roles, there is a reality we want to acknowledge, a reality that's seldom discussed: Not all leaders have the same access to mentors and sponsors.

Not all leaders get access to the most important networks. This is especially true for women and men of color. Michael McAfee, president of a national public policy institute and one of the men we interviewed, shared his story that we believe represents this difference well. As an African American man who came from a working-class background, Michael's perspective is drawn from his own rise up the career ladder, as well as from having mentored dozens of young professionals. Michael saw firsthand that the lack of access to (or sometimes knowledge about) certain networks meant he sometimes was at a disadvantage. He had to find other ways to build the relationships he needed to advance his career.

He notes that white men are raised at a very early age to think about networks and mentors and sponsors. They may not use those specific words, but the socialization of white boys—through sports teams, fraternities, and service clubs like the Boy Scouts—leads to powerful relationships and lifelong connections as men. These affiliations are culturally engrained. They are expected. When white men enter the workforce, they often have these dependable relationships in place and can leverage them; they may have used these very relationships to land those early jobs in the first place. If you don't have an understanding early in life of how these relationships work and why they matter, you are at a disadvantage.

"I've watched white men go after certain positions even when they are not fully prepared. Other white men take them under their wing. These relationships aren't just transactional. They have true mentors and sponsors. That's what helps white men. They move up quicker because they have people backing them up, saying they are ready (even if they really aren't). Our [people of color and women] networks are often very weak," explains Michael. "We aren't plugged into affinity groups. If you are first generation or grew up poor or working class, you don't even know about these networks. You don't know how they work. So, many of us just don't have this background where we learned to socialize in this way. We are learning this on the job when we need these relationships most. And that's what makes it difficult."

It's within this context that this chapter provides practical advice to shorten your learning curve and help you understand and unlock the power of these relationships.

Mentors

Mentors and sponsors are both forms of *developmental relationships.* As we mentioned at the beginning of this chapter, CCL's ongoing Lessons of Experience research tells us that developmental relationships are the second largest sources of development (after challenging assignments) for both men and women[2] and across cultures.[3]

It's common for women and men to be advised to find a mentor. How many times have you heard that? Mentors are great for providing advice and coaching. Most of the women we interviewed offered examples of mentors who had given them strong guidance and support during their careers. Jan Capps, for example, spoke about one of her first managers who taught her good writing skills, saying, "I can't underestimate the importance of that. He taught me to write as simply as possible to make my point. He was also a really good finance guy and helped me build those skills. And when I was frustrated about something happening at work, I knew I could go to him to talk it through. He would listen and give me good guidance."

Marcia Avedon, chief human resources and communications officer of a diversified, global industrial manufacturing company, told us about a manager who had high standards and gave her very good, honest advice. "She'd give it to me right between the eyes, but because I knew she cared about me, I knew it was for my own good."

Jan's and Marcia's experiences with mentors align with the advice that Tim Rice, a retired CEO of a large hospital system, provides to the women he coaches. He recommends that they seek strong mentors—men and women—who will invest time and effort toward helping them develop and advance. He says the ideal mentor is someone who is thinking about that woman's career and development regularly and is willing to give constructive, direct, and honest feedback.

Women can run into challenges when seeking mentorship from men when male leaders are uncomfortable with the "whole person" type of mentoring that women may be seeking. Cam Danielson, CEO of an HR consulting firm, reflects on his early days as a manager. Cam observed that while men typically sought guidance and development using an action orientation and focusing on facts and figures, women generally approached their development from a more balanced perspective that included feelings and the "bigger picture." In the past, Cam says, "I wasn't comfortable with the approach my female team members were taking. It wasn't my strength, so I got quiet. My silence came across to them as criticism of their questions and ideas, which led them to withdraw and be less engaged in the dialogue. That is unfair to the women because I wasn't meeting their mentorship needs. Today I understand this much better, and I appreciate the need for a balance of the masculine and feminine approaches in the workplace. The truth is that both men and women have them, but we start out favoring one over the other. Mentors need to be aware of the impact of their own biases on the people they are fortunate to mentor."

Have you heard the statistics showing that women are over-mentored and undersponsored?[4] It's true that women tend to receive more mentoring than men. Why is that, and is it helping women in their leadership journey? A look at the research suggests this: Women may need (or seek) more mentoring because mentors provide them with the support that builds their self-confidence and encourages them to do some of the things that women tend to do less often and less comfortably than men—such as negotiate,[5] promote themselves,[6] and apply for stretch assignments or positions.[7] They may also be told to find a mentor while men are directed to sponsors.

Mentors certainly play a critical role for women, but they don't provide the specific support that is often required for career growth. That is where sponsors come in. It is possible to find both mentorship and sponsorship in the same person, but this is not always the case.

Sponsors

Beyond mentoring, sponsors play an additional role by advocating for developing leaders. They recommend that up-and-coming leaders take on challenging assignments, and they actually provide or recommend them for those opportunities. Sponsors are important for men, but they are critical for women. Yet men are more likely than women to have sponsors. Why, you ask? Great question! Let's think about who the sponsors are likely to be. If they are able to advocate and create opportunities for those they sponsor, they have some level of authority in an organization. They tend to hold positions in the upper levels of organizations. If the pool of leaders at the upper levels of organizations is made up of more men than women, men are more likely to serve as sponsors. And because men tend to be more comfortable mentoring and sponsoring other men versus women, well, you can do the math.

Stephen Gerras is a retired Army colonel and current faculty member at the US Army War College. We asked him what advice he has for women trying to move up the organizational ladder. In addition to taking advantage of women's leadership groups in their organizations, Stephen places a great deal of value on the role and value of developmental relationships, and he recommends that women seek out men as mentors and sponsors. But he isn't naive. He acknowledges there can be suspicion of male-female mentorship relationships that creates real challenges to implementing them. Yet he believes most effective leaders are professional and can properly handle such a relationship. Resources such as *Athena Rising*[8] provide useful guidance for women and men who are interested in navigating (and avoiding) potential complications of opposite-gender mentoring and sponsoring relationships.

Marcia had that opportunity early in her career. When she was in a fairly junior corporate HR role, she had a sponsor who was one of the business presidents in her company. He involved Marcia in his business operations and included her in meetings with other senior executives. "Even if I was playing an advisory or facilitative role in the meeting, I learned so much by hearing the conversations. He was doing it very deliberately to develop me. He put me in positions of responsibility that were beyond my own self-concept given my career level and age. I realized I was capable of more than I thought because he thought I was! He respected my intellect and work ethic and entrusted me with very important decisions and projects. He stands out as an important sponsor and mentor."

Tim recommends that women (and men) seek sponsors who can open doors for them. "One young woman I am working with—I can help her and open doors for her," Tim says. "She also has an official coach who is helpful in leadership skills and other areas, but can't open doors. Because she is interested in community leadership, I've also recommended that she find a sponsor who is a woman leader in the community—someone who has walked the path she wants to follow and can open doors for her there."

Rosalie, a university president, has a lot of go-to people that she speaks with constantly. For deep advice, she can go to a few people in her network, depending on whether her need is personal or work-related. Some of the best guidance she received was from someone who has been one of her key sponsors. Rosalie was asked to consider a role at the administrative level of a large university system, but her goal was to become president of a single university. She was hesitant because she felt the systemwide role would take her out of her desired path to a presidential role. Her sponsor shared a story from his own experience that helped her realize the value of a more central role—the exposure Rosalie would get to the many campuses within the system and the chance to work with outside interest groups, the governor's office, and legislators would give her a level of experience she wouldn't gain from a single university campus, even if she were president. In agreeing to take the systemwide role, Rosalie gave herself the perfect training ground for ultimately taking a presidency role. The influence of Rosalie's sponsor enabled her to take a risk that she didn't initially see as valuable.

Networks

While women may have several mentors and perhaps a sponsor or two, a third type of developmental relationship may also be available to her—a network. Think of a network as a connection of relationships both within and outside of your organization. Network relationships may be less personal and close than a good mentor or sponsor, but they also provide access and contacts that can go well beyond your immediate connections.

Networks tend to be *operational*, *personal*, or *strategic*.[9] There may be some overlap in the membership of your networks, but the three types have different strengths and purposes. Operational networks are generally useful to help you manage responsibilities internal to your organization; personal networks support you in your development; and strategic networks focus you on potential new opportunities and provide you with access to the key stakeholders you'll need to pursue them.

We've learned that leaders with good networks:

- Hear new information early and are able to capitalize on opportunities that require merging of disparate expertise and insights, often are promoted more rapidly, enjoy greater career mobility, and adapt to changing environments more successfully[10]

- Are likely to be in an organization's top 20 percent of high performers[11]

- Are more influential in complex corporate structures and organizations (boosts performance by 75 percent)[12]

Some of the women we interviewed are what research by our colleagues Chuck Palus, Vered Asif, and Kristin Cullen-Lester would identify as "network-savvy" executives: they have developed a network perspective that gives them five key advantages over those with more narrowly focused relationships.[13]

They understand how the organization really works. They look beyond the organization chart and seek to understand how information flows through the complex web of relationships within and across departments and levels.

They identify, develop, and leverage hidden leaders. They seek out the informal leaders within the organization and are better able to identify change agents, influential actors, and connectors.

They understand and strengthen their own personal network. They actively analyze their own network, along with the opportunities and constraints it presents, and they make deliberate choices to strengthen it.

They see the organizational network as diverse and changing. They are able to see how different parts of the organization are connected and how to manage those connections.

They foster a leadership culture of interdependence. They know that networks depend on the culture of the organization. If the leadership culture is authoritarian, then leaders can block the free exchange of information. If the culture encourages participative leadership, then networks tend to be well connected and interdependent.

Rosalie says, "As I'm putting together my network, I'm thinking, 'Where can I leverage or make connections for my university, or where can I develop my interests and network?'" So she serves on the board of her local business organization to connect with the business community. She served as chair of the association in which her university is a member so that she could connect with other universities, and she is the vice chair of her community's presidents' group, which helps her connect with other presidents in her area.

Rosalie is frequently asked to be involved in women's networks and is as selective and purposeful with those choices as she is with her other connections. For example, Rosalie says she was once asked to run a women's group in her state, and she said she'd be happy to do it if it were productive for the women involved. Rosalie says, "The group was supposed to be for senior leaders but had evolved into a more junior group that was unable to focus beyond the barriers they were facing to identifying ways to address them. I brought in vice presidents and presidents, and we made a difference there. I only served on it for three years because I thought someone else should take it over, but I want to do things where I'm making a real difference."

Dana Born, a retired brigadier general (USAF) and current university professor, has three people she considers her current "personal board of directors." She tries to spend time with each of them at least every six months for both her personal and professional goals. Dana's network is *diverse* in the sense that these three people come from different parts of her life and *open* in that they don't know each other; they don't meet as a group. Dana benefits from each of them in different ways, based on their own experiences and networks.

One of Dana's network members is retired military and a former boss. "He was the presiding official at my retirement. When I went through some of my most challenging crucibles, he helped me through the storms," she says. "I had worked for him at several different times during my career, so he's been a mentor at different levels—in the Pentagon and at the Academy. He's assisted me with questions related to personal goals, professional goals, and through our shared faith perspective. The second person I consider a key network tie is someone I met in my current role at an academic institution. I have multiple areas of professional overlap with this person and see him regularly. We talk about the organizational dynamics of our university department, about our professional roles in teaching and studying leadership, and about the experiences he's learned in combining his business acumen and faculty practitioner perspective in a university setting. He sees and knows all of my warts, from a business perspective and a faculty practitioner perspective. The third key person in my network was a leader in our state's Women's Forum, which is part of the International Women's Forum—a network of more than 6,500 professional women from around the world in 76 different forums. I don't know how she did it, but she put together a dinner of several amazing women and we sat around saying we are long-lost sisters—we were mothers, mountain climbers, runners, and driven professional women. It was a fascinating night! I felt I had a social support network, but it also became a network within a city in which it is at times very difficult to feel welcome, difficult to get involved in the state and local government," Dana says. "She's very different from me in some important ways, and we differ in our personalities. People ask me why we get along because she is incredibly direct, whereas I am more reserved. But I love it because I need someone who is that 'rough.' She got me further engaged in the organization by asking me to work with her when our state hosted the international conference the following year, and subsequently she asked me to join the board and then become board president at the state level and serve on the president's council at the international level. This network has helped me in so many ways. My passion is using my own network to help others. What I love to do is to create networking opportunities that might not happen otherwise."

Gender Differences in Networks

A recent study by CCL colleague Kate Frear and her coauthors, Alex Gerbasi and Leann Caudill, used network approaches to understand whether men and women differed in whether they identified themselves as leaders to others, and whether others would agree that those individuals were their leaders. To confirm leadership status, a leader and his or her followers would need to share the same views of their relationship to one another. Men overstated their leadership status more than women did, meaning that men were more likely to claim their identity as leaders, even though the people they identified as their followers did not view themselves that way. Women did not overstate their leadership status.[14]

In any network, there are multiple roles that perform different functions (see Figure 4.1). Our colleagues Kristin Cullen-Lester, Chuck Palus, and Craig Appaneal have described these in a CCL publication.[15] We will focus on two of these here to reflect gender differences observed in practice. The first role is *broker*: people who bring together parts of a network or organization that would otherwise be disconnected; they are in unique positions to drive or block change and innovation. The second role is *connector*: those who have direct access to a large number of people in their network; they have great access to information and also disseminate it to others. The difference between the roles is crucial because broker roles lead to more opportunities than connector roles do. Brokers often gain new perspectives because they operate between the perspectives of different groups. Brokers are exposed to information earlier and more often than connectors, and they have access to the creativity and innovation that's inherent in bringing different groups and perspectives together. Brokers are often in the right place when new career opportunities come up.

A former colleague of ours, Chris Ernst, has studied networks and helped organizations to develop theirs. Chris says that in his experience in organizations, women tend to play the connector roles more often than the broker roles. Chris sees women work successfully in their networks when they are curious, when they want to know and understand how to make their network work for them. He encourages women to set up regular lunches with

FIGURE 4.1 Key Network Roles

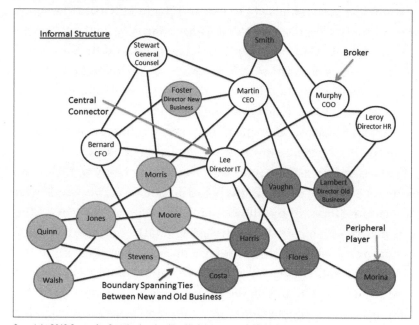

people in the organization, ask questions of those who work in different parts of the organization, and express interest in being part of cross-organizational initiatives.

Research indicates that women are more comfortable devoting time to networking when it serves a purpose beyond just socializing, such as developing new business for their organization or contributing to a social cause that is important to them.[16] They are more motivated and successful in engaging in networks when they are driven by a larger purpose that transcends a specific project and connects with people across the organization who share that same purpose.

Marcia is an example of this motivation for networking. She is active in different associations and boards. Marcia explains her perspective, "What's important is not only that you're a member and on the roster but that you take leadership roles in those

organizations that further the cause of that particular organization. I've gotten a lot of recognition personally over the years
through my commitment to advisory boards, associations, and
other organizations that serve a purpose and allow me to give
back. It comes back to me in many ways. I like doing these things
for the relationship building and the contribution, but it gets me
networked in ways I don't even anticipate."

When asked whether she notices gender differences in terms
of networks, Marcia notes that women are less likely to promote
themselves into leadership roles. "I'm getting ready to finish my
four-year term as the chair of a board, and none of the people who
are coming forward to self-nominate are women," she says. "The
few people who have called me to ask about the role are men. They
seem savvier about it and more intentional about getting to the
goal they want. I think sometimes women think, 'I'll get noticed
and good things will happen; I don't need to promote myself.'"
Marcia considers herself lucky in that people have recommended
her for roles. But she doesn't think women can rely on nomina-
tions. They need to put themselves forward as candidates for the
roles that build networks. They need to act with the agency we
described in Chapter 2.

So far in this chapter, we have shared leadership stories
illustrating the critical role that strong mentors, sponsors, and
networks play in building a leader's exposure, experience, and trajectory. We've shared research reflecting that women experience
these developmental relationships differently than men do. Now
the question is, how are you doing? What does your network look
like? Let's find out!

EXERCISE: WHAT DOES YOUR NETWORK LOOK LIKE?

There are numerous ways to examine your network. CCL uses this
process in some of its leadership development programs.

Step 1

Think of the key stakeholders in your network. They may be mentors, sponsors, your boss, peers, people on your team at work, or people in your broader professional community outside of your organization. Think about people you rely on to help you make tough decisions, get work done efficiently, find the next interesting work or projects, and recognize your work and the work of your team. They may rely on you for any of these needs as well. Make a list of those names.

Step 2

Transcribe your list of names to the diagram in Figure 4.2, or draw a similar figure in your journal. Put your name in the center circle. Then using the concentric circles to show the depth of your relationship with others, put the names of the people on your list whom you rely on most and who may rely upon you most heavily in the next circle out. In the second concentric circle, write the names of people with whom you have a good relationship, although it is not as close as your relationship with those in the

FIGURE 4.2 Network Diversity Graph

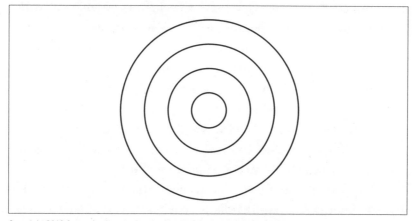

previous circle. Continue that pattern: as your contact with and reliance on people in your list decreases, write their names farther out in the diagram. If people in your network are connected to each other, write their names closer to each other than to others to whom they are not connected.

After you've transferred the names to the diagram, draw circles around the names. Draw a line from each person to your name. Then draw a dotted line between people who are in *each other's* network. Don't worry if your diagram is getting messy—most networks are! Now take a look at your work. When you look at the clusters of people who seem to be connected to each other, do you have some clusters that aren't connected to other clusters at all or perhaps connected through only one person? Or is everyone in your network connected to everyone else? Are all of your network connections showing up in the circle closest to you or in the one farthest away? Or are your connections spread across the diagram?

Now you can use your diagram to evaluate the health of your network. An ideal network would show that you have connections across all of the rings of the diagram—some to whom you are more closely connected and some who are more distant, but still in your network. How many people have you included in your network? Does it feel to you like it is large enough to help you be connected where you need to be, but not so large that managing it is a burden? How connected are the clusters in your network? There should be some connection between your clusters, but the clusters should not be completely connected. When everyone in your network is connected to everyone else, your network is "closed" or "insular," meaning you probably don't have enough good sources of diverse information available to you. We can't give you a specific checklist to know whether your network is diverse. The question is whether you feel it provides you with access to different sources of information and opportunity.

If your network diagram doesn't show the diversity you'd like, fear not! There are a number of approaches you can take to diversify your network—let's get to work.

DIVERSIFY YOUR NETWORK

CCL designed its evidence-based network approach explicitly to help leaders diversify their networks.[17] CCL's work in this area provides information and strategies for diversifying networks to first-time managers, high-potential leaders, managers of managers, and executives. Because *Kick Some Glass* is targeted to midcareer women leaders who are likely to be advancing to manager of managers and executive levels, we will focus on strategies of interest to those levels in this chapter. (You may read about the full set of strategies in the CCL white paper cited.)

Manager of Managers Level: Creating Strategic Relationships

As your responsibility increases in scope and scale, success measures increasingly depend on your ability to execute on strategy and to manage resources. That's true for anyone managing other managers, managing functions and divisions, and managing entire organizations. These leaders form the operational hub of the organization and are constantly torn by opposing stakeholders and revolving priorities. They are swimming in requests, action items, deadlines, meetings, and performance requirements. As a result, the need for a strategic network increases in importance. And that's a big shift in how many leaders manage relationships. As a reminder, strategic networks focus you on potential new opportunities and provide you with access to the key stakeholders. A strategic network needs to be diverse—to identify new opportunities and access to different key stakeholders, it's critical for your network to provide you with insights and connections from different areas and types of sources.

As managers move from managing individual contributors to managing other managers, the key change they experience is a lack of independence. Organizations provide high-potential leaders more freedom for taking on initiatives and getting things done. Strategic leaders no longer have this independence. Managers of managers—those leading in the middle zone of the organization—must serve their executives and their own people, translating requests from the top to the bottom and from the bottom to the top. Leaders of divisions or functions must mesh their visions with the organization's vision.

The lack of independence and the focus on execution often drives leaders to build networks of people who can "get stuff done." Leaders who are managing other managers have very little time or energy for mistakes, so they often don't feel that they can take risks by trusting people who are not known to them. Their natural reaction is to surround themselves with people who reliably respond and execute. But there's a real danger in doing that. Relying on people you know and avoiding people you don't in your preoccupation with execution may cause you to neglect strategic, future-oriented relationships. Those strategic relationships (mentors, advisors, strategic business partners, career coaches) are what you need to thrive in the manager-of-managers role and to make it to the next level.[18] Even when leaders know they need to network more strategically, they often feel they don't have time. They are caught between strategy and execution. If you can do both, you will succeed, as Marcia did. She was intentional about including in her network several people who were two levels above her in past roles and organizations. She was able to provide unique contributions to those relationships because her background and skill set were different from those of her managers, and she gained insight into how business operates at the senior executive level—a perspective that she wouldn't have been exposed to otherwise.

It only takes one or two deep strategic ties to make a difference in your success. It's important that you periodically evaluate your network and determine if relationships are tactical or strategic (if they focus on execution of current needs rather than on more holistic, long-term needs), immediate or long-term (available for your current needs or for your long-term needs), surface or deep (familiar with only certain aspects of your needs compared with your holistic needs). Create and maintain at least two or three relationships that are strategic, long-term, and deep with people who will help you understand and achieve your business and career objectives. Also build relationships that are tactical, immediate, and surface.

Some ways to connect strategically with others include:

- **Reach out to colleagues in the same role to begin building strong ties with your peers.** They are likely experiencing similar issues and are important to accomplishing goals that span organizational departments or functions.

- **Ask for business advice.** Learn to lean on others. Seek out advice from experts outside your field to understand how they relate to your job. Get the perspective of others who have managed similar projects or problems.

- **Seek career advice.** Don't go it alone. Find a coach, mentor, HR advisor, or other person who can give you a perspective on the big picture as well as help you figure out what you need to do to be ready for opportunities that may come along.

- **Connect others.** Introduce two people who should meet each other. Let them know they each have information, ideas, or insight the other would find useful.

- **Help a contact get a job inside your organization.** This creates a tie for you in another area of the business.

- **Delegate more operations to your employees.** You may need to coach and develop individuals as they take on these tasks, but it is essential if you are to work at a more strategic level.

Executive Level: Reversing Insularity and Isolation

As you move from a manager-of-managers role to an executive level, your world changes again. Life in the C-suite comes with full responsibility and accountability. Senior executives must create strategy for the organization and manage multiple stakeholders and audiences. Developing strategy requires these top leaders to find organizational and political support for their ideas. At the same time, they must manage their public image and the image of their teams. CCL research finds that the ability of an executive to drive strategy effectively across the organization is tied directly to his or her image in delivering key statements around the organization's goals.[19]

Networks play a significant part in an executive's ability to manage these dual efforts (galvanizing support and promoting an image) and to encourage direction, alignment, and commitment throughout the organization. The key change leaders will experience as they transition from being a manager of managers to the executive level is to manage the overwhelming organizational pressure for performance and intense personal image scrutiny. At this level, every action or nonaction is watched by the board, peers, direct reports, and other employees. Competitors also are watching for signs of stress, overload, and uncertainty. These C-suite executives must be "on" at all times, assessing whether or not their actions and words are being understood, reinterpreted, or misrepresented.

The predictable influence on networks under these circumstances is to let the pressure and image scrutiny drive you to work only through proven relationships. You've cultivated these trusted relationships over many years, and you know they are dependable and reliable. These relationships provide a buffer zone for the executive and serve as an extension of the executive.

Your primary network goal in these circumstances is to reverse the insulation and isolation that long-term relationships can cause. C-level leaders tend to circulate among themselves, and they also hold back and shape the information they share. The CEO is insulated, and the whole executive team is likely to be experiencing similar isolation. In addition to determining whether you need to build and activate new relationships that are strategic, deep, and long-term, and whether any existing relationships are not as valuable to you as they were in your previous leadership level, it's a good idea for you to look at the network patterns of your executive team as a whole to determine what relationships are present and valuable and which are missing. Marta Grau, HR director at a global publishing company, takes the approach of mentoring one or two less experienced leaders every year. By including them in her network, she is hearing things that she wouldn't otherwise hear from people at her level and is able to integrate what she is learning into the strategic work for which she is responsible. Break insularity and isolation using these strategies:

- **Consider your image.** What habits and behaviors may contribute to your isolation? What can you do differently to end that isolation?

- **Tap into your latent network.** Assuming you have minimized focus on your previous network relationships in a positive way that leaves people open to connecting more strongly now, look for previous contacts and relationships that you can revive or reenergize.

- **Spend time at a start-up within your business sector.** Get unfiltered access to people and information.

- **Schedule skip-level meetings to get unfiltered information.** Find ways to talk to people throughout the organization and factor their experience into your decision making.

- **Attend a conference you have never before attended.** Step out from your current circles of colleagues and the same pool of information.

- **Be a guest speaker at a local or national event.** These experiences push you out of your established patterns and open the door to new relationships and ideas.

- **Find a personal network assistant.** Use your staff to find interesting and new people inside and outside your organization to invite for short informal meetings—be curious, understand their world, and follow up if you find something interesting.

- **Introduce two executives at the same level who do not know each other.** Use your position to help others make valuable connections. Your behavior can start to shape and strengthen networks throughout the organization.

WHAT ABOUT THE QUEEN BEE?

Inevitably, as we work with midcareer women who are trying to build their networks and relationships with sponsors or mentors, we will hear about the "queen bee." She is usually described as a high-achieving woman in the organization who could be so helpful to other women if she'd actually support them but seems to intentionally get in their way instead. Is the queen bee real, and if so, why does she exist?

Our colleague Sophia Zhao paired up with other researchers to find out. They asked, "Is it possible that senior women leaders are unwilling to support other women leaders because doing so could unfairly penalize the senior leaders?" The answer is fascinating. When women are perceived by their peers to value diversity, they are rated lower on leadership competency and performance by their bosses. Men's bosses, on the other hand, rated men who were perceived to value diversity higher on both leadership competency and performance.[20] In a second part of the study, women leaders who advocated hiring a woman over an equally qualified man because they wanted to "increase organizational racial and gender balance" were rated as having less competence and lower performance than if they advocated hiring a male candidate. Men leaders, on the other hand, were not penalized for wanting to hire the woman candidate.[21]

As a woman, what can you do about the queen bee phenomenon? First, be aware of gender bias. If you see a woman who is acting like a queen bee, speak with her about supporting other women. Then walk the talk and give her your support. If you are that queen bee, understand why you are potentially treating other women unfairly. Seek support from your network to be a champion for women while still being a champion for yourself. Second, be a vocal and visible advocate for creating an environment where both women and men are treated fairly according to their strengths. And finally, champion diversity and inclusion in your organization. Engage men in doing so as well. The responsibility for developing policies, practices, and mindsets that shape a diverse and inclusive workplace lies with both women and men.

QUESTIONS FOR REFLECTION

Use your journal to reflect on how you can use some of the tactics we just shared to connect strategically with others and reduce insularity and isolation. Here are some questions to get you started:

- Which peers should I build a stronger relationship with? Who can help me access diverse parts of the network?

- Whom could I seek out for business and/or career advice?

- Is there someone I can help to find a job or connect with a contact who can help them in some way?

- Where can I step into a new arena, such as an association in my industry or a networking event I've never attended?

- How can I build visibility for myself to people two or more levels down in my organization?

Developing relationships with mentors, sponsors, and networks is something that women and people of color are less likely to do naturally relative to white men. We hope this chapter helped you change that. Go and build *your* network of champions.

Beat the Impostor Syndrome

Sometimes I would feel like this job is over my head.
But you have to be a little scared. If you feel like the job
is a piece of cake, you aren't challenging yourself.

—Susi Takeuchi, Chief Human Resources
Officer, UCLA Health Sciences

In this chapter, you will learn:

- How to recognize if you are prone to the impostor syndrome
- Four high-impact steps you can take now to banish the impostor syndrome and fully own your success

'm a big phony. There is no way I'm qualified for this job. They just felt sorry for me. I have no idea how I got here; I'm just lucky. Have you ever had these thoughts about yourself? Do you dismiss your accomplishments? Do you fear that at any moment you are going to be found out and your career will end? Have you turned down opportunities because you didn't feel ready or were afraid you would make a career-limiting mistake? In Chapter 2 we talked about conscious and subconscious mental models that can hold us back. For some of us, those mental models are about not truly believing we are worthy of our achievements despite our hard work and credentials.

You aren't alone. In our research and in our coaching conversations, we've seen high-achieving executives crippled by self-doubt, feelings of being a fraud, deep insecurities, and limiting beliefs—hallmarks of what is known as the impostor syndrome. I (Portia) suffered from a full-blown case of it.

Working in Shanghai as a public relations executive was a big promotion for me. But from the moment I arrived nothing seemed to go right. During my first week my new clients told me they were unhappy with the firm and were planning to take their business elsewhere. I had to do something. I couldn't fail at this job.

So I went into overdrive, working day and night to save accounts and rebuild the relationship with clients. I worked crazy hours and went without sleep. I stopped eating right. And the whole time, I waited for the other shoe to drop. I asked myself, "What am I doing here? How long before people realize I have no idea what I am doing and I completely flame out?" I told myself I wasn't cut out for the job and I should never have taken it. On and on these thoughts ran through my head.

Gradually, the firm's accounts improved and clients stopped threatening to pull their business. But even then, I felt that the stress and pressure of the situation was killing me. I worried constantly. I lost weight. My hair started to fall out. One night, the company's CEO called to check in. I was sure that he was calling to fire me. Wrong. He'd called to commend my performance and to see if I needed any additional support. That call should have brought me a wave of relief, but instead it drove me further into the depths of self-doubt. "Oh my God, they are watching me in New York!" I thought. "Now I really can't screw up."

At the time, I had no idea that I was experiencing the impostor syndrome. And years later, when I gave a TEDx talk titled "Why a Successful Person Feels like a Fraud," I was overwhelmed by the response of audience members.[1] Many approached me afterward to share their own stories of feeling like frauds.

The impostor syndrome was first described by Pauline Rose Clance and Suzanne Imes in 1978 as *impostor phenomenon*.[2] It occurs when successful and intelligent professionals don't feel like they deserve their accomplishments and that they have faked their way to success. Since its introduction, impostor syndrome has been well researched and documented. People who suffer from it experience negative stress, fear, and anxiety, lose confidence, and become averse to taking risks—not a recipe for a successful career.

Sue Cole, a retired CEO in the finance sector and now an executive coach, says she has experienced imposter syndrome all her life. She remembers once giving a speech to 2,500 people, some of whom approached her afterward and complimented her on her poise and confidence. But they hadn't seen her sick in the bathroom just three minutes before the speech! "I never had a high level of self-confidence and always felt like an imposter," she says. "I didn't think I was good enough and couldn't figure out how I got to where I was." Sue can afford to be philosophical about her past feelings now. "It probably caused me in the long run to come off with more authenticity, to try harder and to prepare more."

Sue recognized her imposter syndrome struggles, but we see many women who don't realize that is what they are experiencing. A closer look at these women reveals many commonalities: They are goal-oriented overachievers. They often rack up big successes early in their careers. During their careers, many were the "only one"— the only woman or person of color, for example—and believed (even if not objectively true) that they stood out or were subject to extra scrutiny that their male or white counterparts didn't receive. As a group they crave achievement and success, but it often comes at a high price. These women talk about feeling like they weren't worthy of their promotions or status. It's plain that they have risen through a series of roles with progressively more influence and rank, but they often feel they are one mistake away from losing it all or from humiliating themselves, revealing their phoniness.

These women also talk about the career opportunities they turned down for fear of failing. Some admit to workaholism, micromanaging, overpreparing for even the most minor of assignments, or seeking perfection to avoid making mistakes. Here's what we have learned about these women: Your willingness to step out of your comfort zone and stretch (and we mean *really stretch*) is directly proportional to your ability to grow beyond your current role and skill set. It helps to have what Carol Dweck calls a growth mindset.[3] If you build your tolerance for mistakes, even failure, the knowledge, capability, and growth you experience as a result will propel you further than if you stayed snugly cocooned in your comfort zone.

Confidence, which is undermined by the impostor syndrome, comes from having a clear sense of your worth, your unique contribution, and your purpose, and from the knowledge that perfection and freedom from mistakes isn't the goal—growth is. You control your destiny. You decide how fast or slow you go in your career. How you reach your goals is up to you. Embracing these notions takes on added significance in the face of the impostor syndrome. (Previous chapters in this book urged you to exercise your intention and develop a sense of agency. Both are key defenses against the impostor syndrome. If you skipped them to get here, we encourage you to go back and review them. It's worth it.)

SYNDROME FIGHTERS

In our conversations with women, we met several from whom we can learn answers on how to fight the imposter syndrome.

Abeer Alharbi, the Saudi nuclear physics professor, had never even heard the term. "When I fall down, I have more energy to stand up," she says. "Failure and challenge are both fuel for me to succeed." Susana Marin, the general manager of a luxury hotel in Spain, also never has experienced the imposter syndrome. "There is something unique in each person. When choosing a leadership position, or going through the process to get a position, you must be true to your best self. I know many other people could have been in my same positions and done a wonderful job as well, their way."

Both these women possess a degree of self-confidence, fortitude, and awareness that guards them from the impostor syndrome. How about your perception of yourself related to those qualities? Who else in your life seems authentically confident? Ask them if they've experienced the symptoms of impostor syndrome. What can you learn from them?

GIVE YOURSELF A BREAK

To get over the impostor syndrome, you first have to cut yourself some slack. The process of becoming who you are supposed to be is just that—a process. Give yourself permission to screw up. You can't grow and improve unless you take some chances. The more chances you take, the more likely you are to screw up. That's just the math. Focus less on achievement, superficial markers of success, external rewards, and other people's opinions, and you will free yourself to soar and stumble toward the life and purpose you intend.

DO I HAVE IMPOSTOR SYNDROME?

Earlier in this chapter, we noted a number of telltale signs of the impostor syndrome. Let's consider what you might see, feel, or do if these signs are symptoms of impostor syndrome.[4]

- If you tend to assign equal weight to every task and see everything as high stakes, you are apt to **overprepare**.

- If you avoid situations where you think you might fail or where you're not 100 percent sure you know everything about what you are supposed to do, you might **hold back your talents and opinions**.

- If you have a hard time advocating for yourself to get raises, promotions, and choice assignments, then you might **keep a low profile**.

- If you wait until the last minute to work on important projects, **procrastination** could be a sign of impostor syndrome.

- If you have a hard time recovering from a setback or failure, your **lack of resilience** may indicate impostor syndrome.

FOUR STEPS TO OVERCOMING IMPOSTOR SYNDROME

If you recognize any of the tendencies we just described, you're not alone. Many women (men too, for that matter), act against their own interests when affected by impostor syndrome. But you can fight back. Here are four tactics that can help you in that fight.

Focus on Facts

When you are asked to list the successes you are most proud of, do you struggle to articulate your accomplishments? Do you dismiss your achievements as dumb luck or a result of external forces? Completing a personal success inventory can help you discover your strengths and express your success. To help you get an objective perspective on your accomplishments, consider challenges and assignments you have carried out and record your achievements in the personal success inventory in this section. You will also find this exercise on www.kicksomeglass.com.

PERSONAL SUCCESS INVENTORY

CHALLENGE OR ASSIGNMENT	DATE	ACCOMPLISHMENTS	SUCCESS DRIVERS: SKILLS/ CAPABILITIES/ PERSONAL QUALITIES THAT HELPED YOU SUCCEED

People under the influence of the impostor syndrome often don't give themselves enough credit for their accomplishments. They attribute their successes to luck, hide behind their teams, or credit external forces that have little to do with their own talents. Look objectively at your record of success (this is where the personal success inventory comes in handy), and you are bound to see that your success isn't an accident. There is a pattern to your accomplishments. If you remain unconvinced, then take some time to look at your past performance reviews or revisit your most recent 360-degree ratings, if your company uses them. (Look in your bottom desk drawer. That's probably where you shoved the survey and promptly forgot all about it.) You might be surprised at what your colleagues give you credit for but you dismiss. Are you great at building a team? Can you bring simplicity to complexity and chaos? Can you inspire people even in the midst of extreme difficulty? These are gifts! But many of us suffer from what is known as "negativity bias."[5] Negativity bias occurs when we give negative experiences more weight than those that are positive. Negativity bias explains why we remember (and often ruminate on) traumatic experiences. In our coaching engagements we've observed that while men are quick to tell you what they are good at (good for them), women can struggle to articulate and own their successes and too often dwell on failures. And we get it. As we will note in Chapter 10, in many cultures young girls are socialized to be modest, deferential, and self-effacing. To some men (and even women), there is something a bit scary about a woman who will stand out there on her own to tell you why she's so damn good and why you should pick her. But you've got to get over that. You are your own best advocate, so step out there and be proud of what you have done. Your company isn't paying those people to butter you up. Take them at their word—especially those whom you know to set high expectations. They above all others are unlikely to treat recognition of good work lightly.

Challenge Limiting Beliefs

Negative beliefs about what it takes to succeed, the outcomes of failure, and how self-worth is measured are often at the root of impostor syndrome. Success, real success as you define it for yourself, isn't based on pedigree or background. Some people get a head start, for sure. They are born to wealthy families. Their skin color is favored by the culture they live in. Their path to the best education is eased by connections. But the rest of us aren't destined for the loser's bin. Regina Hartley's insightful TED Talk describes why someone whose life is characterized by abundant adversity is a better hire than someone who has had abundant opportunities. Hartley shares her own story of growing up in poverty as the fourth of five children to a father who was severely mentally ill and a mother who had to raise her and her siblings alone. Despite the odds, she put herself through college and went on to have a successful career in human resources. Hartley's advice? Bet on what she calls "the Scrapper," that person who was able to leverage her or his hardships to fuel a deep sense of purpose and passion. "In spite of everything and against tremendous odds, they succeeded," she says.[6] The Scrappers in Hartley's story didn't limit themselves to shortsighted beliefs. Neither should you.

Do you have limiting beliefs about what it takes to be successful? What do limiting beliefs look like, sound like? Are these familiar?

- "I'm the first person to graduate from college in my family. I could never get a job in that industry."

- "That company has never had a woman in the C-suite. I could never aspire to rise that high."

- "There's never been a person of color that senior in the company. There's no way I can compete for that job."

Limiting beliefs can hold us back from realizing our true heart's desire. They can keep us from taking the risks we need to take to get to the next level. But that doesn't need to be true for you. April Miller Boise didn't let limiting beliefs stop her. Now general counsel and corporate secretary for a global diversified industrial company, April remembers her days as a young law student and her realization that she was, in fact, as good as her fellow students, regardless of where she had gone to school.

April attended a large, public state university as an undergraduate and then a prestigious law school. She remembers that first-year law school students had a brochure that showed where the students went to undergrad and where they were from. She noticed that most had come from small private schools and had attended small private high schools. "I remember someone saying, 'Oh you went to a public school,' implying, *How did you ever get here?*" April said that even if other students didn't use those words, their intent was clear from the tone of their voices and the looks on their faces. She remembers thinking, "I went to public school. Am I questioning myself because I went to public school?" (Of course, she had no idea whether other students were also doubting themselves as well!)

Public school wasn't the only thing that made April feel like an outlier. So did the fact that she was an African American woman. She remembers that when she went for her first summer law internship, just after finishing her first year of law school, there were about 40 summer interns. In that group there were probably six women and very few minorities. She found herself wondering whether she could cut it at law school or the firm.

April realizes how ridiculous her thoughts were in hindsight. "I look back on that situation now and think, 'You were perfectly fine! You were just as qualified as, if not more so than, all of the people there.' But when you are the only one, when you stand out, you always feel like the exception." From her present position as a successful corporate attorney working at the highest levels in her profession, April sees that she had everything her private school–educated classmates had and more. Her experiences back then insulated her later in her career from feeling inadequate, and they encouraged her to own her accomplishments and have confidence in her knowledge and experience. She never held herself back from pursuing the opportunities that fulfilled her career ambitions. She relishes that she can walk into a room—whether or not she is the only woman or person of color—and feel comfortable about the skills and experience she brings and the value they add to a situation.

If you suspect that limiting beliefs hold you back from realizing your success, take a few minutes to think about April's story: from public school to a top-tier law school, where most of her classmates came from elite private schools. Her drive, ambition, and work ethic (not to mention the "public school chip" on her shoulder) led her to graduate at the top of her class, to land plum summer internships, to get her first post-law-school job, and to build the successful career she has today.

We met Susan Tardanico, a former chief communications officer turned entrepreneur and leadership coach, in Chapter 3. She was willing to reflect on her prior successes, which helped her step outside her limiting beliefs. Susan initially didn't think she had what it took to be a corporate officer when offered her dream job. She looked at other corporate officers and was convinced she didn't have the right qualities. She had the drive, but she wasn't actively managing her career other than preparing herself for when she was offered an executive position. She was so bent on preparing for the moment that when the moment came, she tried to decline her own promotion! Shocking? Yes. Surprising? Not really. We know from experience that feelings of being an impostor can be very powerful and can potentially derail one's career.

Susan remembers the incident clearly. She had relocated to London and was working on a team tasked with transforming the company for which she worked. By this time, she'd spent the better part of 15 years saying that she didn't want the top job but wanted to be ready for whatever came her way. One day she traveled to Washington, D.C., at her boss's request. "It was all shrouded in mystery," she says. "I actually thought that I was being sent to her office to be fired. I went through a mental inventory of every possible thing that I had done wrong." Susan entered her boss's office, and her boss slid a press release across the desk. Susan, shaking, thought it was either a resignation letter or a separation package. Instead, it was an announcement that she was being named chief communications officer—a hefty promotion. Fighting back a wave of nausea, her first thought was, "I'm not ready." So she thanked her boss and said she just wasn't ready, didn't yet possess the skills to handle the job. Her boss was incredulous. "Are you out of your mind?" she asked. "Are you kidding me?" Susan did accept her promotion, of course. She says, "Looking back on it now, I can't believe that I felt that way. I didn't see what I was bringing to the party. I didn't feel worthy. I didn't feel that I was officer material. I believed that the other officers were more capable, more expert. But after I lived it for a year, I realized I could do it," she says. Susan now recognizes the limiting beliefs that almost kept her from achieving the highest-ranking position in her field. "I thought I had to be something else—something more—to qualify to be an officer," she says. "In my mind, that was an entirely different kind of leader." Susan admits that her initial reaction was also linked to fear. "I actually did have the skills," she says. "Maybe I was afraid of failing because the position made me visible. I was one of only four women in that echelon. Every move those women made was watched by 40,000 employees."

Claim Your Strength

People living with impostor syndrome are their own worst critics. They tend to overemphasize their faults and play down what they do well. We've seen plenty of women obsess over negative comments in a 360-degree feedback survey and completely overlook the positive feedback that's right in front of them. If we point to the positives that their colleagues attribute to them, they'll wave off the praise and say, "Yes, but look at what they say I don't do well!"

Sound like you? Consider this: If you don't recognize what you are good at, how will anyone else? And if you don't tout your skill (more on that later), why would anyone seek you out for challenging, rewarding assignments? If you aren't on your own side, who is? There will be times in your career and personal life where you'll be called to forcefully advocate for yourself. Will you be ready to say why you are the only one who can lead that project or take on that newly created role? Will you be able to say at a moment's notice what unique gifts and talents you bring that no one else can?

It can be hard to talk about where you excel. We've struggled with that, too. In many societies, girls are socialized to be kind, generous, and self-effacing. They're taught that modesty means not talking about yourself (no one likes a smarty-pants show-off, right?). Well, we're here to tell you, don't be afraid to be powerful and fully embrace all that makes you so damn good. When you recognize and own your strengths, you radiate a personal power that is uniquely yours.

Jabu Dayton has certainly claimed her power. She's a successful HR consultant to some of the world's most successful start-ups, including Airbnb and TaskRabbit. You might not have seen that potential when she was young. Her parents didn't tell her she was dyslexic. She was a shy, nerdy kid. Now she thinks those qualities give her a special affinity for engineers and for people outside the norm. She likes—even prefers—people who color outside of the lines. She doesn't care if she's talking to a well-spoken Harvard graduate. "I'm able to appreciate the outsider because I was the outsider. I am an African, first-generation American, mixed kid. I grew up in Seattle, which at the time wasn't diverse. Early on, I figured out I wasn't going to fit in, so I went my own way," she says.

Jabu emphasizes nonconformity as a strength. It's important to her that she let other women and non-gender-normative people know that she didn't fit in, either. She sports tattoos that people can see—it's part of her brand and a sign that she's not your typical HR person. When you work with Jabu, you're working with different. "In the early days of my business, when I interviewed with different start-ups, I would go in wearing a T-shirt and jeans just to see if I would get the job," she says. "I went in with pure Jay-Z swagger, and it worked really well with the elite start-ups. It created a certain kind of currency that I started to use. I built a brand around being a nontypical HR consultant."

Jabu didn't always carry that swagger. Early in her career she assumed others knew more or brought more skills to her profession than she did. She recognizes now that when she was young she actually tried not to be powerful. Like many girls, she grew up under influences that told her she had to be pretty, polite, and appropriate. "People who have power don't worry about these things," she says. "I've learned this lesson in growing my own personal power."

Take a page from Jabu's notebook. How can you flip what you perceive as a liability into a strength? From a perceived liability—a dyslexic, shy, multiracial girl growing up in a homogenous community where she didn't fit in—Jabu forged her own sense of identity and personal power. She flipped her perception of liabilities into a recognition of assets that allowed her to relate to Silicon Valley clients. She understands what makes tech entrepreneurs tick, and she uses that to make deep and powerful connections with her clients. It's a unique, successful approach that she built herself.

Talk About What the Impostor Syndrome Does to You

People living with impostor syndrome often feel like they are the only ones who feel they way they do. That's not hard to understand. It's difficult for most of us to share our vulnerabilities with others. No one wants to look bad or unable to handle the pressure of our jobs. We take pride in our competence and believe that any feelings of doubt or insecurity make us weak. Not true! Talking about your feelings and experiences is exactly what you need to process and put them into perspective. Sufferers of the impostor syndrome are frequently shocked to learn that people they know and admire often have the same feelings. What we've learned from the women we've coached and worked with is that the impostor syndrome isn't a permanent condition. You *can* get over it.

I (Jennifer) offer my own story as proof. I learned the term *imposter syndrome* during my first semester of graduate school. During an orientation class required of first-year graduate students, I worked with Dr. Frank Landy—the most senior faculty member in the department and a significant leader in the field. Anyone studying or working in the field of I/O psychology knew who Frank was because he had written multiple books, was highly respected in the field, and testified in numerous legal cases due to his expertise. So you can imagine my shock when Frank admitted to having imposter syndrome. "I worry on a regular basis that someone will say they made a mistake awarding me my PhD and that I have no business influencing students and others in the field through my work," I remember him saying. I never forgot that exchange, although it took on different meanings over the course of my career. I share my own sense of imposter syndrome with others in hopes they will, also, feel less alone and isolated.

When I started at CCL, I was hired by the vice president of research for a project he needed someone to staff. I was not competing with a slate of candidates for a posted position. I got my initial interviews through my network, was hired on contract for a specific project, and within six months was hired to be a full-time employee. Talk about imposter syndrome! The messages that went through my head were, "I was hired through the back door; there wasn't even a position. I didn't have to go through the same selection process that other researchers do." On and on and on.

I have been exceedingly successful in my work, but the imposter syndrome followed me for many years—about 20, to be exact. But then I went through my first full selection process for the job I currently hold. Before that, I was promoted based on my strengths, accomplishments, and potential, yet still felt like an imposter until the first time I went through what I hadn't experienced when I first joined—a competitive selection process. If my experience resonates with you, I encourage you to use some of the lessons in this chapter to crush your imposter syndrome and believe in yourself by seeing that others believe in you. Don't let it take 20 years to be convinced that you are NOT an imposter!

EXPLORE YOUR IMPOSTER SYNDROME THROUGH REFLECTION

As you've learned from the stories in this chapter, even the most accomplished people can feel like frauds. The impostor syndrome is real, but it doesn't have to define you or derail your career. What is most important is that you recognize the signs and symptoms and know that "this too shall pass." Know that, when you are stretching and challenging yourself, there are going to be moments (long ones even) when you feel like, "What the heck am I doing? I don't belong here!" Rather than running from that, embrace those feelings. Get curious about why you are feeling the way you are. Here's what we've learned from the executives we spoke to and the women we coach: You are more ready than you know. You have more talent than you may recognize. Feelings of fear and inadequacy are normal in the face of new challenges and new ways of working when you are striving to align your intentions with your actions. Trust yourself. Trust that all you have done before will serve you well. Trust that you are ready. Now grab your journal and reflect on these questions.

Maybe you worked your way through college and graduate school. Maybe you're the first in your family to get a college education. You might have grown up poor or with a single parent. Perhaps you are first generation, the daughter of immigrants. The list goes on. What lessons have these unique life experiences taught you that perhaps others haven't learned? Have they made you more tenacious? More resilient? Able to read a room with uncanny accuracy? Think about those lessons when you notice limiting beliefs creeping into your thinking, affecting how you act and the choices you make.

If you didn't do it earlier, make notes about your limiting beliefs, and go back and look at your personal success inventory. Ask yourself the following questions:

- How have my previous successes allowed me to counteract those limiting beliefs?

- Looking back on my career thus far, when have I most felt like an impostor? What lessons have I learned from that time that I can use now or in the future? How can I flip my sense of being an imposter into a reflection of my strengths?

- Do I still have limiting beliefs that are holding me back? What lessons can I glean from this chapter to help me address those beliefs?

- Whose observations of my strengths, accomplishments, and potential do I trust? How can I ask for their honest assessment of me?

CHAPTER

6

Get Fit to Lead

Actively make time to work out. It's that important.
Be healthy and well enough for the whole marathon.

—JoAnna Sohovich, CEO of the
Chamberlain Group

In this chapter, you will learn:

- How to crush stress and sleep like a baby
- The effects of not getting enough sleep
- The importance of the morning routine and bedtime ritual
- Strategies for building your resilience

The executives we interviewed for this book are overwhelmingly committed to their overall well-being. They didn't all start out that way; many discussed crucial turning points in their lives that made them examine their lifestyles and habits. Sometimes there were personal health crises, but just as often it was the illness of a spouse or parent that made them take stock of their own health. For some, having decreased parental demands as their children aged gave them more time to focus on themselves. Others are still in the process of shifting from *knowing* their own well-being is important to *doing* something about it.

When we planned this book, we knew we wanted to include a chapter on health and fitness. But we didn't want to just give conventional advice about eating right and getting enough exercise. You already know about those things. We wanted to approach health and fitness as strategic decisions for designing the life you want and enhancing your longevity.

In his book *The New Leadership Literacies*, the Institute for the Future's Bob Johansen writes:

> The tools for energy management are so much better now than they ever were—and they will get even better over the next decade. Leaders will have no excuse now. Fitness will be the price of entry for top leadership roles.[1]

The women we spoke with already understand Johansen's claim. Almost all of them talked about their carefully considered lifestyle choices. Not every woman we interviewed was a hardcore athlete or nutrition fanatic, but they had thought carefully about what activities fueled them and unlocked their energy reserves. They had learned to listen to their bodies and feed them to sustain that energy, to provide mental focus, and to support their longevity.

Our interviews didn't uncover any magic formula for well-being. But we did find a lot of experimentation with activities and food combinations to find something that worked. For example, Rosalie, a university president, told us she felt healthy in her twenties to her early forties, but then realized she needed to do something differently. "It's about weight, but it's also about eating better and exercising, and finding a place for that in my life," she says. These executive women sometimes consulted experts, such as personal trainers, nutritionists, and therapists. Other times they researched on their own (after all, we are talking about highly motivated goal-oriented women here!) and experimented until they found a solution that felt right. They were, as a group, keenly tuned into their bodies and how they felt. They knew when they weren't getting enough sleep, eating enough of the right foods, or stressing to an unhealthy degree. And they learned to calibrate to attain something close to a sense of balance and well-being.

Women face a complicated challenge when it comes to health and wellness. Many of us are mothers caring for children, and sometimes we are also caring for aging parents. And we face the complexity of hormonal swings added to the changes in metabolism that accompany aging. The women in our interviews and the CCL survey data are high achievers with demanding jobs. We are the COOs of our home—meaning we often handle most of the major tasks related to the home front despite our crushing responsibilities at work. The 2017 "Women in the Workplace" report by LeanIn.org and McKinsey & Company, which confirms that women are still doing the lion's share of the housework, may resonate with you. The report found that 54 percent of women say they do all or most of the household duties compared to only 22 percent of men. And the report goes further:

> This gap grows when couples have children. Women with a partner and children are 5.5 times more likely than their male counterparts to do all or most of the household work. And even when women are primary breadwinners, they do more work at home.[2]

What particularly surprised us in the report's findings was that even women who are primary salary earners or in senior executive roles still do a disproportionate share of the housework!

The report goes on to conclude that because senior executive women (57 percent) tend to be in dual-income households, they don't reap the benefits of a stay-at-home spouse. According to this research, the net effect dampened not only the physical well-being of women but also their career ambitions. Feeling even more stressed out after reading this? We've got you. The good news is there are steps you can take to better manage your competing priorities to stay healthy and fit.

IT STARTS IN YOUR HEAD

In her research conducted with thousands of senior executives, Sharon McDowell-Larsen writes about the importance of sleep, proper nutrition, and exercise for overall wellness and optimal brain health. In her article "The Care and Feeding of the Leader's Brain," she pinpoints four key areas to boost your brain health: sleep (our personal favorite); exercise, which she calls the "magic bullet"; feed your brain; and counter the effects of stress.[3]

But how can we possibly have time to eat well and get enough sleep and exercise when the demands of daily life are urgent? How can we approach this "wicked problem" in a way that is practical *and* sustainable over time? We'll explore part of the solution in this chapter and take up this pressing issue of home front management in the following chapters.

WORK IT OUT!

If you work out regularly, you're familiar with the benefits of exercise. Regular exercise has a significant impact on mood, including alleviating depression and anxiety and increasing feelings of optimism. It turns out exercise is also important for brain function. Regular exercise induces a process called angiogenesis (the creation of new blood vessels) in the cerebellum and motor cortex.

These new blood vessels keep the brain nourished and promote proper oxygen and nutrient delivery. That helps the brain to rid itself of toxins and waste. The link between exercise and brain health is becoming much clearer as data becomes available about the causes of dementia, Alzheimer's disease, and other brain disorders.

The women we spoke to are time starved and busy. (Aren't we all?) But they are also achievement oriented, curious, and eager to share what was working for them and what they wished they had known earlier in their careers. JoAnna Sohovich, CEO of a US-based manufacturing company, brought her lifelong dedication to fitness from her days at the US Naval Academy, where 97 percent of the incoming class are varsity athletes.

So how does JoAnna do it? It's simple, really. But even a simple system demands discipline. "I have a reccurring invitation on my calendar to go to bed at 9 p.m. I wake up early enough to be ready for a 5 a.m. workout. When I was younger I could short sheet sleep. But not now," she says. Did you notice her bedtime? So did we. In fact, we were surprised at how many executives credited their mental performance to getting enough sleep.

CAN WE TALK ABOUT SLEEP?

We never thought we'd see the day when sleep would become a lifestyle movement, but we are thrilled that public figures like media mogul Arianna Huffington are bucking the trend of leaders bragging about how little sleep they get. In her 2010 TED Women talk, Huffington recalls her moment of truth. One day, while clocking yet another marathon day in her office, she fainted from exhaustion, hit her head, and broke her cheekbone. She subsequently went on a mission to overhaul her life and share her lessons more broadly in what she called a "new feminist revolution." She panned the idea of the lack of sleep as a sign of virility. She mused whether the financial crisis might have been avoided if leaders behind the companies like Lehman Brothers had gotten more sleep instead of existing in a state of perpetual connectivity. After she extolled the benefits and virtues of sleep she proclaimed that it was women who were going to "sleep their way to the top," modeling what it was to be a well-balanced (and well-rested) leader.[4]

Turns out, Huffington was ahead of her time when it comes to the sleep zeitgeist. The National Sleep Foundation (NSF) recommends adults age 24 to 64 get seven to nine hours of sleep per night.[5] Yet in a recent CCL study, leaders reported getting 6.63 hours a night. Among these leaders, 31 percent reported difficulty sleeping. Leaders in this study reported that they needed 7.52 hours of sleep to feel rested. Yet only 14 percent of them reported getting 8 hours or more of sleep; 44 percent reported getting 7 hours; 32 percent reported getting 6 hours; and less than 10 percent reported getting less than 5 hours.[6]

Nearly one in four leaders in CCL's survey said thoughts about work were keeping them from getting a good night's rest. This same CCL study showed there was also a gender component to sleep. Women tended to report that worry about life and work events interrupted sleep. Not surprisingly, this study showed that women reported more sleep debt—about 68 minutes—meaning women feel more sleep deprived.

This didn't surprise us. A 2015 study from the Working Mother Research Institute surveyed more than 1,000 dual-income families, which revealed what many working moms already know: they do it all—including scheduling doctors' appointments, arranging play dates, buying birthday gifts, planning school lunches, not to mention handling household chores.[7] While the number is gradually declining, women are primarily responsible for the "second shift." Put it all together, it is no wonder women report feeling sleep deprived.

The benefits of sleep are clear. Sleep helps memory and cognition. Emerging evidence indicates that toxins, such as those associated with Alzheimer's disease, clear from the brain during sleep.[8] Not surprisingly, adequate sleep is also associated with good decision making and creativity. And it probably won't surprise you to learn that longevity and overall physical health are also associated with good sleep hygiene. So how can you get the sleep you need—not just what's adequate but restorative? We looked to science and bolstered what we found there with what worked for the women we interviewed.

Getting the Sleep You Need and Deserve

Try some of these strategies. Some will click, while others won't. As our interviewees taught us, keep trying until you find what works for your body and lifestyle.

Make your bedroom your sanctuary. Many sleep experts advise that you use your bedroom only for sleep and sex, yet for many women (men, too), the bedroom is an extension of the office. If you have kids, you may find your room has become a de facto family room, strewn with toys and games. Make a commitment to keep your bedroom only for sleeping and intimacy. As sleep has become a lifestyle trend, luxe bedroom decor has become equally popular. You don't need an *Architectural Digest*–level overhaul to make your bedroom a place you look forward to each night. Declutter your night stand and dresser. Invest in good-quality light-blocking shades and curtains. A high-quality mattress is a must; most mattresses outlive their useful life after 10 years. Make sure yours is supportive so you don't toss and turn. Top it with high-thread-count sheets and a beautiful duvet or comforter in natural fibers. Whether you prefer down or synthetic pillows, make sure they support your head and neck for good alignment during sleep. Finally, and this is important, take the TV out of your room! Make your room a haven of peace and quiet that upon entry signals it's time for you to relax, unwind, and prepare to end your day.

Set a specific bedtime. Many of the women we interviewed were recovering night owls. As Selma Miele, an advertising executive put it, "I discovered that as I got older, I just couldn't stay up as late. I had to go to bed early to function the next day." Bedtimes varied from as early as 9 p.m. to as late as midnight. On average our interviewees reported 10 p.m. as the bedtime sweet spot.

Untether from all electronics. We know it's easier said than done in our hyperconnected world. We get it. It's tough to peel away from your phone and television. We use our devices for work and to wind down—absentmindedly scrolling through our feeds or channel surfing from bed. Use the hour before bed to read a paper book or write in a journal to gently unwind your brain and set the stage for sleep.

Sleep in a cool, darkened room. According to the National Sleep Foundation, 65 degrees is the ideal temperature for a restful sleep. Minimize all blue light in your room, including phones, alarm clocks, DVRs, and other electronics. As the day goes on, the cells in the retina register dwindling light and trigger the brain to produce the hormone melatonin, which lowers body temperature and gradually reduces alertness to induce sleep. Ambient blue light from TVs and other electronics interrupts this, disrupting your natural sleep process.

Try white noise. We have fallen in love with the sound machines (they aren't just for babies anymore!) in our hotel rooms on business trips to block out strange sounds or uncomfortable silence. Think about getting yourself one for your bedroom. If sound machines bother you, use a ceiling fan or a humidifier instead. You're looking for just enough of a gentle buzz to filter out random sleep-blocking sounds.

Go easy on the booze and heavy foods. Learn which beverages and foods disturb your sleep. Sleep experts agree that consuming caffeine late in the day can disrupt sleep. But consider that nightly glass of wine—it may initially make you drowsy, but it may also be the culprit in preventing you from maintaining continuous deep sleep. Avoid greasy, heavy, and spicy food too close to bedtime. Eating right can be hard if you travel frequently for business. The executives we interviewed all reported maintaining a strict diet on the road, focusing on clean proteins and vegetables in lieu of heavy meals, and limiting if not abstaining from alcohol completely during weekdays. JoAnna, the manufacturing company CEO, always travels with protein bars and tries to eat light during her frequent business dinners on the road. When I (Portia) travel for business, I go online, look up the menu of the restaurant where I'm planning to eat, and select my dinner option in advance so I'm not tempted to make poor food choices.

Have a consistent bedtime routine. If you have or have had kids, you know how important it is to keep them on a consistent bedtime routine. Maybe you gave them a bath followed by reading them a story every night. Perhaps you briefly snuggled under the covers before lights out. Repeating that pattern night after night ensured that your child knew it was time for bed when the routine started. This same principle works for adults. Try unwinding with a hot bath or shower. Liv Santos writes out the next day's priorities as a way of emptying her head and preparing for rest. Many read fiction right before bed. In fact, one executive laughed and noted it could take her weeks if not months to finish a book because she frequently fell asleep while reading.

AND HOW TO WAKE UP

While we were interested in the sleep habits of the women we interviewed, we were equally interested in their morning routines. We wondered, What did they do first thing when they woke? What did they do second? How did they set the stage each day to be productive? And of course we wanted to know what the research said about the morning rituals of high-performing individuals.

The women we interviewed had varying routines, but the one common denominator we found with almost all of them is that they worked out in the morning before they did anything else.

Like sleep, the importance of the morning routine is a serious news and social media phenomenon. The Internet is awash with advice for starting your day. A simple scan of one of our favorite social sites, Pinterest, turned up over 100 pin boards on morning routine advice. You can find advice that seems like a good fit for you by checking blogs and health sites. Our advice is always to follow what works for you. To help you get started, try one of these and see if it works for you (try one for a week or so before adding or moving onto another one).

Wake up early. The most productive professionals reported waking up no later than 6 a.m., and many rose as early as 4:30 or 5 to make sure they had time to exercise and weren't sidetracked later in the day.

Hands off your phone. Tempted to grab your phone and scroll through your e-mails immediately upon waking? Don't. The executives we spoke to almost universally agreed that checking and responding to e-mails first thing in the morning tended to derail their mornings, so they abstained unless absolutely necessary.

Get moving. Exercise was the most preferred activity for the women we interviewed. They reported their morning workouts as essential to their sense of well-being, focus, and productivity. On average, they exercised for a minimum of 45 minutes most days of the week.

Meditate to focus the mind. We were pleasantly surprised to learn from the executives we spoke with that they used mindfulness practices such as meditating, reflection, or journaling when they woke.

Express gratitude. Wake up each morning giving thanks. What are you thankful for? Friends? Your loyal dog? The health of your family? You need not be religious or even spiritual to give thanks. By tapping into your sense of gratitude, you open a wellspring of positive energy that will emanate from you throughout the day.

Find your intention. The Upanishads, an ancient Hindu text, says, "You are what your deepest desire is. As your desire is so is your intention. As your intention is so is your will. As your will is so is your deed. As your deed is, so is your destiny."[9]

So often we focus too much on what we are not going to do or what we hope doesn't happen. For 30 days, try focusing on your intention(s) for the day. It could be as simple as not to engage in mindless snacking or to listen without distraction.

Keep a journal. If you journal, you will join the ranks of luminaries including Benjamin Franklin, George Lucas, Barack Obama, and Oprah Winfrey. Journaling has become de rigueur for business executives looking to minimize stress, organize their thoughts, fuel creativity, and tap into their emotions before the day begins. As we researched this chapter, we were struck by the profundity of such a relatively simple exercise to transform one's thinking and attitude. Journaling, or "morning pages" as author and artist Julia Cameron calls them, is a deeply personal exercise in letting go. Cameron's rationale is that petty, angry, and childish emotions cloud our minds, clutter our subconscious, and block our creativity. When we get them out on the page, we free ourselves and allow our creative selves to emerge. Cameron's morning page advice, written over 30 years ago, still feels fresh as we strive to find tranquility in our hyperconnected, frenetic world.[10]

Marta Grau, HR director at a global publishing company, told us about her morning ritual: "I get up early in the morning and have an hour to myself. I write a little bit, I think about my day, I have coffee. I'm really relaxed with my notebook where I write a little bit every day about what I'm happy about and what worries me."

A final word about morning routines: You might have noticed that we said nothing about eating breakfast. Many of the leaders we interviewed were breakfast eaters, but just as many were not. Some preferred their first meal closer to lunchtime. One leader we spoke to is a devotee of intermittent fasting (IF), a method of fueling the body that involves cycles between fasting and nonfasting to drive weight loss and sustain energy throughout the day. Breakfast has been called the most important meal of the day, but the science of whether it's best to eat or wait is debated.[11]

BUT WHAT ABOUT THE NIGHT OWLS?

You've read this advice on waking up early to the morning routine, and maybe you are thinking, "Nope. That's not me." You may be in the minority of people who are natural night owls. We aren't talking about the folks who force themselves to stay up late to crash on a project. You just naturally go to bed late. We know these folks. They do their best work in the wee hours of the night when the rest of us are sound asleep. Sometimes they need very little sleep and can wake up early, or they've chosen professions (techies, designers, and those in media and entertainment) that allow them to structure their work so they can shape their hours to fit their needs.

We love the advice that appeared in a *Fast Company* article, "How to Thrive as a Night Owl in a World of Early Birds."[12] Among the pithy pieces of advice, the article suggests asking for flexibility to work from home one or two days a week if you have a long commute that forces you to get up early or to change your work hours, say from 10 a.m. to 7 p.m. rather than 8 a.m. to 5 p.m.

As with all our advice, do what works for you. If you are a night owl who needs only five or six hours of sleep, go for it. But we encourage you to listen to your body. Sleep when you are tired, and when you do sleep, use the tips we've discussed to make sure you are getting the highest quality sleep you can.

STOP DIETING AND STRIVE FOR LONGEVITY

If most of us (except for you night owls) aren't getting enough sleep, many more of us have eating habits no better than the average college freshman. We drink too much coffee, eat too many processed foods, consume too much sugar, and take in too many carbohydrates. The result? We feel sluggish. Our brains fog late in the day, and we have uncontrollable cravings that we quell with carb-laden food that only increases the cravings. It's easy to go from diet to diet, sometimes with success, only to backslide, sometimes regaining the weight we lost.

CCL's senior executive program, Leadership at the Peak, has an entire section devoted to health and fitness.[13] At the beginning of the program, executives receive a comprehensive fitness evaluation that includes blood work, family health history, and an overview of lifestyle risk factors. Yet while many of us have the best of intentions (we certainly fit the bill), we know that many of us are wary of esoteric diets and complicated workout routines. We are busy women, and we need pragmatic solutions that help us eat better, keep our heads clear, promote a sense of well-being, and provide energy to do the things that matter most to us. When it comes to food, accepted medical advice now says we should strive to eat more whole plant foods such as leafy greens, fruit, nuts, and beans. One of the women we interviewed, Abeer, offers her own insight: "Food is a nice gift from God. I don't have much time to enjoy things, so when I have good food, I enjoy it." There is a lot to be said from taking joy where we can find it!

THE BOTTOM LINE

Strive to exercise most days of the week. It doesn't matter what you do, just move—even as little as 10 minutes a day. Make it a goal to stand more than sit. Try a standing desk. Try wearing a biometric device for ongoing feedback about your activity level. Strive to eat a balanced diet where fresh vegetables, fruit, nuts, and seeds are the core, and lean meats are not the focal points of your meal. Reduce stress by nurturing your relationships and cultivating a sense of community around you.

The Blue Zone project provides some compelling evidence for these recommendations. You may have heard about Blue Zones, those places in the world with high concentrations of centenarians: Okinawa, Japan; Nicoya Peninsula, Costa Rica; Barbagia region of Sardinia, Italy; Ikaria, Greece; and Seventh-day Adventists in Loma Linda, California. The term *Blue Zone* was originally coined by two demographers, Gianni Pes and Michel Poulain, who shared their research about these regions of unusually healthy centenarians. *National Geographic* fellow and writer Dan Buettner used this research as the basis for his bestselling books *Blue Zones* and *Blue Zone Solution*. Researchers studied these Blue Zones to distill why people in these geographies seemed to outlive their counterparts around the world. In these regions people had astonishingly low rates of heart disease, dementia, and diabetes. How do they do it? Researchers discovered that daily exercise, plant-based diets, nurturing relationships, and the occasional glass of wine (sign us up!) contributed to longevity in these regions.

We loved the Blue Zone research for its focus on longevity and its highly doable and holistic approach to healthy living. There are plenty of online resources if you are curious to learn more. You can start your journey at www.bluezones.com for a wealth of information on the research and local resources.

CULTIVATE RESILIENCE

Within their insights about health and performance, the women we interviewed stressed one other addition to sleep, waking routines, proper diet habits, and regular exercise: resilience. What is resilience? CCL defines it as strength amid change and stressful life events. It's the power to spring back from adversity.

Life being what it is, there will always be times when we experience difficulty at work. How can we become more resilient in the face of adversity? Diane Coutu says that resilient leaders have three defining characteristics: a clear acknowledgment of reality; a deep belief centered on values that hold life is meaningful; and a talent for improvising. You can bounce back from hardship with just one or two of these qualities, but you will only be truly resilient with all three.[14]

My (Portia's) experience is a poignant illustration of the importance of resilience. After the birth of our first son, Gideon, when I was 40, my husband and I decided to start trying for a second child a year later. That led to two years of roller-coaster secondary infertility. While pregnancy came relatively easy, keeping those pregnancies did not. Each pregnancy ended between six and eight weeks. The last miscarriage came on the heels of a tragic loss in my family.

On the advice of a friend who had lost her father to suicide in her early teens, I sought professional help. While I wasn't always comfortable feeling vulnerable, I shared what I was going through with close colleagues and family. With the support of my counselor and community, my feelings of helplessness began to fade. I began to feel more optimistic about the future. And to my surprise, the resilience I learned in my personal life carried over into my professional life and enabled me to more effectively manage stressful situations.

We don't have to experience personal tragedy to develop resilience. In *Work Without Stress*, Derek Roger and Nick Petrie describe what drives stress and how to build resilience.[15]

The key to battling stress? Stop ruminating, according to Roger and Petrie. We are all guilty of it. Thinking about something over and over again without resolving it. Rumination creates elevated levels of adrenaline and cortisol, both associated with the body's automatic fight-or-flight response to duress. Long periods of rumination can lead to a weakened immune system, increased inflammation, and less productivity because it interferes with mental focus and clarity.

Roger and Petrie list four steps to building resilience, which are also closely aligned with the concept of mindfulness:

1. **Wake up (and stay awake).** Be present and mindful of your surroundings. Observe your behavior throughout the day. How often do you zone out? Try to maintain as much of your attention as possible.

2. **Control your attention.** Building on your state of wakefulness, practice controlling your attention. It will take time, but as you practice, you will be able to hold your attention for longer periods of time.

3. **Detach.** Learn how to put things in perspective. People who ruminate often obsess about things over which they have no control. Learn to not sweat the small stuff. Worry less about things you can't control.

4. **Let go.** Learn to stop fixating on things that aren't important. Focus on the bigger picture, and when you find yourself "in the grip," ask, "Why is this important to me? Am I unnecessarily worrying about this for no reason?"

To see where you fall in terms of your capacity for resilience, complete the short exercise at the end of this chapter.

As women with multiple competing priorities, we know there are never enough hours in the day. Most of us know what we need to do, but struggle to find the time. Something else always finds its way to the top of the list before we can take care of ourselves. If you read this chapter and are doing most of what we've outlined, good for you! Keep up the great work. If you are like most of us and could use a lot more sleep, a bit more exercise, and perhaps just a wee bit more discipline around your diet, you are not alone. Start with incremental changes in areas where you need help most and where you know you can sustain the change. We promise you'll love the results you see.

A final thought: We really liked Heather Banks's approach to staying focused on her health in spite of her hectic schedule. A chief human resources officer based in the mid-Atlantic region, Heather has worked hard to get to a place where her mind and body are in sync. She's a working mom to two school-aged kids and is keenly tuned into what her body needs. In addition to keeping a regular workout regimen and watching her diet, she pays equal attention to her mindset. She says, "What I have been trying to embrace is, How do I just own who I am? What choices am I making? Am I going to be planful, or am I going to be a victim of what is there?" Her hard-won discipline includes regular visits to a reflexologist and massage therapist. Especially important is her faith. She is a practicing Catholic and is raising her children Catholic. "It's a beacon for me. My faith grounds me and allows me to reflect and connect," contributing to her resilience and sense of balance.

REFLECTIONS ON YOUR HEALTH

In this chapter we've shared some best practices and strategies for your overall health and well-being. Take some time to consider these questions in light of your own health and wellness strategies. Grab your journal and write down your thoughts.

- Am I happy with the amount of sleep that I am getting? What is one thing I can do every day to improve the quality of sleep I get?

- What about my morning routine is working well and contributing to my energy? What is one thing I might change to improve how I start my day?

- What is my honest assessment of my fitness and diet?

- What is the one thing I could change tomorrow that would make a big difference to my health?

Use your journal to list objectives and goals that will start you on a healthier path.

MEASURE YOUR RESILIENCE

Answer true or false to the following questions:

1. When I get upset it usually takes me a long time to recover. **T F**

2. I find myself replaying negative or stressful incidents in my mind long after they have happened. **T F**

3. I am easily distracted and find it hard to focus on one thing for very long before I'm thinking about something else. **T F**

4. It's sometimes hard for me to put things in perspective. **T F**

5. I tend to worry a lot about things that are beyond my control. **T F**

6. It's hard for me to find time to exercise most days of the week. **T F**

7. I find it difficult to eat healthily most days of the week. **T F**

8. It's hard for me to get eight hours of sleep every night. **T F**

Review your answers. If you answered mostly true to these questions, you may want to examine your ability to recover from setbacks. Identify one or two things you can change right now to improve your resilience. For example, can you go to bed one hour earlier to get more sleep? Can you decrease the amount of the time you spend zoning out and increase the amount of time you remain awake, fully present in the moment? Remember, this is a process. Don't beat yourself up if it's hard to change old habits. Even small changes can yield big results over time.

Motherhood: Don't Drop Out, Power Down

Enjoy your personal milestones and take them as opportunities to grow outside of work. It can be a very reflective time.

—Samantha Lomow, SVP Hasbro Brands, Hasbro, Inc.

In this chapter, you will learn:

- The challenges when women try to manage a career and children simultaneously
- Several alternatives to dropping out of the workforce while raising children
- Solutions that free up more of your time at work and at home to focus on what matters to you and your family

There are many difficult choices that women face as they progress on their leadership journey. One of those choices is specifically demanded of women who have children. Whether they carry their children for nine months or adopt, or whether they are parenting alone or with a partner, the addition of children to the equation of a working woman adds a dimension of complexity. Each woman must determine the best way to navigate this part of the equation for herself, her family, and her career. Here's what we know for sure: it's usually doable with planning and foresight.

Anne-Marie Slaughter wrote about her experience and the insights she gained in an article in the *Atlantic* magazine titled "Why Women Still Can't Have It All."[1] Her conclusion was that— at least in the United States today—there are structures, policies, and belief systems that need to change in order to even the playing field so that working women with children have the same opportunities as working men with children. And while this is all very true, those changes will take years. Unfortunately, that isn't very helpful to those of us who are struggling with this tension right now.

This chapter will help you explore your options when motherhood and career collide. We will deal with the impact of motherhood on careers and how to juggle both and still be fulfilled. Key to that balance is to help women understand that motherhood doesn't have to mean shelving your career—even temporarily. In fact, when women "drop out," the penalty upon returning to work shows up in lost wages, lost influence, lost career advancement, and the organization's loss of the talent that returning women bring with them. Those penalties affect not only the working mother but her children, her organization, and a future where we need to see more women in the workplace rather than fewer. Although we are speaking in this chapter about choices related to having children, we are both part of the "sandwich generation" that has responsibility for both their children and their parents. We hope that what is shared here will be helpful for readers tasked with eldercare as well as childcare.

THE CHALLENGES

There are many challenges facing women in the workplace who decide to start or raise a family. At one end is the practical matter of leaving a role for an extended period: weeks, months, or years. At the other lies the cultural expectations and biases about how long women will remain in an organization and whether it's worth developing and promoting them if they might not stay. That range of challenges appears in several specific ways.

Inflexible and Insufficient Leave Policies

More women might stay in the workforce if they had more job flexibility. The US Bureau of Labor Statistics has mapped a drop-off in the number of women in the workforce since 1999, which some analysts blame on the lack of progress in national family leave policy for new parents in the United States.[2] When it comes to the difficult decision of how long to be on leave from their jobs, women in the United States suffer from some of the worst levels of federally mandated leave policies in the developed world, leaving more progressive companies and states to fill in the gaps. Any parent knows how crucial flexibility is, not just when the kids are small but through the teen years. And while American companies are becoming increasingly enlightened, the reality is that it's difficult to work a demanding job and raise a family when the lion's share of child-rearing responsibility is on the woman.

Over the course of our own careers, we've encountered a number of women who chose to leave their careers to stay home to care for their children. Women have many compelling reasons to take time off work, from wanting to be present for their children during their formative years to saving on childcare costs. Because let's face it, when childcare costs outstrip the salary of one parent, it often doesn't make economic sense for both parents to continue to work. Yet some women don't have the luxury of living on a one-parent paycheck, for either the short or long term. Many women are single parents and don't have a choice about returning to work because they are the only breadwinner in the family. Other women simply don't want to choose between building a career and building a family. They want both, which is "allowed" for (even expected of) men.

Other countries and some states in the United States have mandated maternity and parental leave to alleviate some of this burden. At the federal level, there is no such coverage at the time we are writing this book. New mothers must use their FMLA (Family Medical Leave Act) benefits toward their leave, if they even have access to those benefits. Many women in low-level or service jobs do not. Around the world, 185 UN-member countries provide some form of maternity or parental leave. The United States is the *only* advanced economy that does not mandate maternity leave at the federal level.[3] The good news is companies like Google, Facebook, and Microsoft are leading the way toward generous paid family leave policies.

Other advanced economies such as Canada, Sweden, and Norway provide at least 26 weeks of leave, and low-unemployment countries such as South Korea, Japan, the Czech Republic, Austria, and Denmark offer 52 weeks of maternity leave. The International Labor Organization, a UN-affiliated agency, recommends that mothers have 14 weeks of paid maternal leave. Why are we sharing this data? While you may not have the influence to change these practices yourself, being aware of the differences in practices across countries helps you understand the global context of support for family leave and possibly provide some data to your organization for its consideration and action. It may also help you make decisions about where you want to work, potentially setting your sights on a state or company that has already instituted more progressive parental leave policies.

I (Jennifer) took some form of leave after each of my three children was born. I was still in graduate school when Sarah was born in 1992 and spent most of her first six weeks working from home on a research proposal that became my dissertation. On the bright side, I was with her for that time. With Christopher in 1995, I was already at CCL and took the six-week FMLA leave (at 60 percent of my salary) allowed plus two additional weeks at 50 percent while working from home. With Grace in 1999, I took a total of three months—the six-week FMLA leave (60 percent salary), two weeks unpaid leave, two weeks at 50 percent working from home, and two weeks at 50 percent working in the office. I truly appreciated the flexibility I had in shaping my maternity leave in a way that worked for my family and me. Even though I had a reduced salary (or no salary) for this time away, I felt good about being able to stay home longer with Chris and Grace than I had with Sarah. It gave me more time to spend with my older children in addition to the new baby. I also appreciated knowing my job would be waiting for me when I returned and being able to gradually get my head back into work rather than starting immediately at 100 percent.

However, as much as I appreciated the support I was provided, the norm in my world 18 years ago is no longer the norm globally, and women nowadays are demanding better policies. We say good for them! The more men and women call out the need for better parental leave policies, the more likely organizations will retain talented women who would otherwise drop out.

I am very happy to say that CCL has revised our parental care policies to include 100 percent parental medical leave for six or eight weeks for women who give birth (the duration is prescribed by the woman's doctor) and 100 percent parental care leave for four weeks for all employees (women and men) who become parents through childbirth, foster care, or adoption. For women who give birth, this leave can be added onto their parental medical leave, for a grand total of 10 or 12 weeks.

Many of the women we interviewed faced difficult choices when motherhood and career collided. Kecia Thomas, a senior associate dean at a large university, was a junior professor when she and her then-husband wanted to begin a family. With her first child, they tried to time her pregnancy so that she could be off the teaching rotation for a nine-month period after he was born. With her second, the goal was a summer birth to accommodate the fact that the university didn't provide maternity leave. But then things got a little complicated. "I was being recruited to be a department head at another university," Kecia says. "I remember my husband driving me and my son to that university in another state for a two-day interview. I got the position. But they were inflexible about a start date, even though I was clearly pregnant. I couldn't start the role when they needed me, so I had to turn it down. It would have been a great opportunity for career advancement for me. Since then, I have worked with my department to create an arrangement for an intermittent form of maternity leave that allows women to take FMLA for their teaching responsibilities. They still hold and are paid for their research responsibilities, which decreases the impact on their sick leave while maintaining their pay."

For those readers living in countries and/or working for companies that provide meaningful parental leave policies, we congratulate you. IBM, for example, now offers up to 20 weeks of paid maternity leave and 12 paid weeks for fathers, partners, and adoptive parents.[4] Forward-looking policies such as this may reduce the pressure to drop out of the workforce among women during their child-rearing years. However, inadequate leave policies aren't the only challenges facing executive women who are considering starting a family.

Will My Job Still Be There?

Some women are concerned about whether their employer will replace them while they are on leave following the birth or adoption of a child. While US FMLA policies and those in other countries are written to protect the job of the person on leave, the reality is that those policies are unequally enforced and implemented. While Kecia had to manipulate her family's schedule to accommodate her university's policy, women in academic roles in Saudi Arabia, for example, don't face such drastic scheduling choices. "In the university system, a mother will be able to take 45 days at full pay," says Abeer, the nuclear physicist. "She can then choose to take from six months up to three years of leave

at one-quarter pay. Her job is guaranteed until she comes back."
Outside of the university, however, the situation is quite different.
"In the corporate world, she will only have the option of 45 days,"
Abeer says. "She can take more time without pay, but her job won't
be guaranteed when she returns."

There is often weak accommodation for parental and maternity leave through FMLA, but organizational practice may not
bolster that meager support. A woman taking leave for birthing
and childcare may be told that her company cannot do without
someone in the job while she is out so they have a temporary
replacement, but she then learns that the company wants to keep
the replacement in her role when she returns. Or the company
may be able to accomplish its goals without replacing her, and as
a result restructure her work in ways that don't suit her upon her
return. These strategies are illegal, but some companies imple-
ment them anyway. The result is a fear among women that it may
happen to them if they take "too much" time for parental leave.

Reputational Loss

In 2007, sociologists at Cornell University ran an experiment to see
whether there was what they called a "motherhood penalty." Partic-
ipants in the study reviewed job applications from men and women
that were paired by gender (two female applicants, for example).
Each applicant had comparatively equal skill and experience. The
only difference between applicants was their parental status. The
results were eye-opening. Mothers were evaluated as less committed to their jobs than nonmothers, while fathers were perceived to
be more committed than nonfathers.[5] Mothers were deemed less
likely to be recommended for hiring and promotion versus women
with no children. No wonder women feel pressure to return to work
sooner than they'd like to after the arrival of a new baby! Sue, a
retired financial CEO, certainly felt it. "I was the first pregnant person in that role," she says. "I felt the pressure to get back to work. So
I took off six weeks with each of my daughters. Given the seniority

of my leadership role, I don't think I could have taken more than six weeks without it being an issue for my career." However, research by Marian Ruderman, Patty Ohlott, Kate Panzer, and Sara King tells us that the multiple roles a woman holds when she combines parenting and professional work actually make her more effective in her role as a leader, in addition to being more satisfied with life and having increased self-esteem.[6] Unfortunately, many women do not feel that organizations view their multiple roles as a positive thing. Organizations and managers can do more to recognize the benefits accrued by women holding multiple life roles.

Impact on Future Earnings

In the same study as the one that tested reputational loss, researchers looked at the recommended starting salary for hypothetical new employees who differed only by parental status. Mothers were recommended for a lower starting salary than women who were not mothers ($139,000 versus $151,000), while fathers were offered a higher salary than men without children ($152,000 versus $148,000).

Each of these challenges contributes to some mothers deciding that it's not worth it to rejoin the workforce (assuming they have the choice). With so many talented and highly educated women leaving the workplace, nonprofit organizations, educational institutions, governments, and corporations miss out on incredible talent. The problem is amplified by the difficulty women face in returning to the workforce once they temporarily step out. Even those women who are able to reenter the workforce face not only the loss of wages while they were out but the compounding effect of loss of annual pay increases, which keeps them behind men and women who chose not to step away to raise a family. That financial gap can persist over an entire career.

There is, however, another alternative: Women may not need to leave their organizations if they can adjust the demands of their roles to accommodate childbirth and child rearing. They can power down rather than drop out.

POWER DOWN

What does power down look like, and how can it help you maintain your career path when the responsibilities of childcare make sizable demands on your time? Powering down might look like going from full-time to half-time work. It might mean job sharing. Or it could mean dividing a 40-hour week among four days rather than five. It means keeping one foot in the door of the labor force while creating a career that is flexible enough to accommodate your family needs. Two prevalent models of powering down that we've seen are creating flexibility in your current role and stepping completely into a new career.

If you are an employee in good standing, we recommend that you first try to negotiate a more flexible arrangement before quitting. Employers hate to lose top talent, and you may be able to create a schedule that's a win-win for you and your organizations. We both have agreed to several such situations for employees in our own departments, and it's worked beautifully. We were able to retain highly valuable employees, and they were able to spend invaluable time with their young children. Job sharing is one of those options, where two people share the work and salary of the same job, enabling both to stay engaged in the workforce while minimizing the economic burden on the organization.

We've also seen a trend in which women leave their organizations, become independent consultants, and then contract with their former employer while also landing new clients. Employers often like this approach: it enables an organization to retain some utilization of a talented former employee while reducing some of the overhead costs, including full-time payroll and benefits.

Some women have created entirely new careers for themselves. We think this is a smart alternative for women looking to stay in the workforce but who need more job flexibility. When we ask women who chose this option what led them to start their own businesses, invariably the answer is "flexibility and autonomy." But be careful. Going out on your own has downsides. Leaving your job and working as a contractor or consultant means missing out on benefits such as healthcare, flexible spending accounts, and retirement contributions. It means the potential loss of steady monthly income. Be prepared to trade those kinds of rewards for the autonomy and flexibility you need to work around family obligations.

I (Portia) met a female brand consultant who had held executive-level marketing positions at several longstanding, reliable companies but decided to power down her career so she could spend more time with her two children. Over the course of several years, she built a very successful practice working with small and medium-sized businesses. When the Great Recession hit in late 2008, she scaled back her business and focused on her children, relying in part on savings from her consulting practice to keep the bills paid. Now that the global economy is on an upswing, she has more clients and she is able to manage them around a schedule that fits her family life. After my own maternity leave ended, I opted to work from home one day a week. Not only did this allow me to keep breastfeeding my son during his first year of life, it also saved me an hour-long commute one day a week, allowing me more time with my family.

These days, there is more good news for women opting to power down. More companies are taking advantage of the gig-economy wave and using part-time, contract, and temporary services, which means there are far more opportunities to create your own business and build a roster of clients who will gladly pay for your skills and expertise. Take advantage of it!

Some employers don't look favorably on women who voluntarily leave the workforce. All the more reason to reconsider quitting your job if you think you may want to return to work in the future. But if you need other compelling reasons to consider powering down rather than dropping out, here are some ways powering down can help you stay engaged professionally in some way.

WHEN TO POWER DOWN

In our coaching practice we've seen women power down during different times in their lives. Some power down after they give birth to spend more time at home with their baby (or babies) during those early years of life. And here is the thing about pregnancy: you always hope your pregnancy and birth will go well, but complications can happen. You may find you need to recover from a complicated C-section, or perhaps your child is born with medical difficulties. Both are good reasons for powering down. We've seen other coaching clients power down when their children are slightly older. One coaching client's 10-year-old son was diagnosed with a learning disability, and she realized she needed to be around more to coordinate his care. Working with her employer, she negotiated working from home several days a week so she could spend more time at her son's school, as well as take him to specialists. We also shouldn't forget that many women are often simultaneously raising children *and* caring for aging parents. The care of a sick or frail parent frequently falls to women. We have a colleague who took an extended leave from work to care for her mother who was diagnosed with Alzheimer's. When she was able to come back to work, she did so in a role different than the one she had left, but one that suited her needs *and* enabled CCL to benefit from her significant talent and contributions to our organization.

KEYS TO POWERING DOWN

Here are some keys to help you power down successfully.

Maintain Your Competitive Edge
If you've been out of the workforce for a while, employers may not perceive you as being as competitive as other candidates. While

we know nothing could be further from the truth, they might think your skills have become obsolete, that you've forgotten how to work in a team-based setting, or that you just won't work very hard. Whether you've powered down or taken a shorter hiatus, it's critical to keep up with your industry. Regularly read industry news or take a class. Think about your caregiving role as the job that it is; identify the key activities for which you are responsible and the skills you are learning and using. Understand how they are a benefit to an organization. When you are ready to fully jump back into the professional workforce, you will be able to demonstrate current skills and knowledge about the trends and issues driving your field in interviews and networking meetings that may lead to new job opportunities.

Keep Your Network Intact

It's far easier to keep your network intact if you keep your foot in the door rather than shutting the door behind you. School and community volunteer efforts can lead to job leads and contacts, but nothing beats keeping up with your professional network. If you power down your career, maintain your professional association memberships. Attend a meeting or conference every now and then so you can continue to expand your circle of influence. Have regular interactions with the key people in your network, both to remain on their radars and to stay attuned to what they are doing, learning, and talking about. Maintaining an active professional network will pay dividends if and when you decide to go back to work full time.

Ensure You Stay Mentally Sharp

There is something to be said for continuing to challenge yourself intellectually, whether you're formally working or not. The professional women we know who opted to drop out for a few years are incredibly smart, gifted, and talented. To a woman, they all said the thing they missed the most about working full-time was the intellectual stimulation. There are many ways to keep your analytical skills sharp, from volunteering and reading trade publications to part-time consulting, guest lecturing at your local college or university, and staying connected to your professional network.

Outsource Low-Value Activities

Whether you power down or stay fully involved in the workforce while being responsible for child rearing, it's critical to acknowledge that you've added a new set of responsibilities to your role. It's hard to manage it all effectively. Frankly, this is advice for all women—not only women caring for children! Women do a disproportionate share of housework and childcare—the so-called double shift—even at senior levels.[7] Most of the women we interviewed had very proactive husbands, some of whom even decided to let their careers take a back seat to their wives' careers. These women say that partnership with their spouses or partners was key to their success. "I would not have been able to accomplish all that I have in my career without my partnership with my husband," says Samantha, the toy and entertainment company executive. "He enables me to focus my attention on work when I need to and makes it easy for me to transition from work to my family." Samantha and her husband decided early in their careers that she would be the primary breadwinner while he took the reins on the home front and primary care for their two young daughters. Together they ensure that the time she has with her family is quality time, even with the demands of her job. He manages the family calendar, including planning vacations around when she can get away. "It was the right decision for our family," Samantha says. "When our girls were younger we had nannies, but ultimately we decided it was better for everyone if one of us was a full-time presence day in and day out. It's important to stay nimble together because what works for you today may not be what you need tomorrow. Be ready for change."

Joan Tao, former corporate counsel at an international chemical company who joined CCL during the writing of this book, has an interesting way of thinking about the expectations placed on women, especially when it comes to family obligations. She came to her realization through a traumatic hardship, with the sudden and unexpected death of her husband when their children were both under 10 years old. "We have a false notion of a nuclear family—a Norman Rockwell version," Joan says. "I was isolated when I was on maternity leave with our first child because my husband was at work and I was home 24/7 with the baby. In other cultures, I would have had an extended family around me. Women can put themselves in a bind if they begin motherhood with the expectation that they are the primary caregiver and keeper of the home. We've idealized motherhood into a belief that the mother has to be with the child all of the time and that no one else is good enough to take her place. When my husband died, I was so fortunate that my sister was able to come live with me and be a coparent to my kids. She was my hero. I don't know what I would have done without her. But not everyone has that to lean on."

Indeed. But you can lean on other kinds of support. Many of the women we spoke with had come to terms with outsourcing some of the work that is typically expected of mothers. When I (Portia) speak publicly or coach women, I'm frequently asked how I manage my role as an executive, raise two kids, and find time to write and speak. My response is always, "I don't do toilets or floors. I haven't cleaned my own bathroom in 10 years." Wherever possible, figure out what the non-value-added activities in your life are and outsource them. Many of the women we spoke to hired nannies to help with childcare and/or housekeepers to help keep their homes tidy. They take advantage of online grocery services. They use meal-delivery systems or have hired people to help them with meal preparation. Some have even hired house managers to help them coordinate all of these activities. With the many types of services available these days, the ways in which you can outsource support are limited only by the budget you can and want to assign to it.

For many women, however, the budget available to outsource some of the home responsibilities is zero. But there are some creative ways of outsourcing low-value activities. For example, watch a friend's children while she organizes your closets, if she has a talent for it. Ask an accountant friend to do your taxes and agree to bake her family's birthday cakes for a year in exchange. Provide a spare room in your home to a college student who can then clean your house weekly in lieu of rent. And don't forget about the role your partner can play, as well as your children as they get older. A general rule in my (Jennifer's) house is that the person who made the meal is not responsible for cleanup; that belongs to someone who didn't make the meal. This has included our children since they were in the tween ages. Agree to a regular schedule that balances the time spent in homecare and childcare activities with your partner, rather than taking the full burden yourself.

We (Portia and Jennifer) do things differently than our mothers did. We realized that it really didn't matter to our family who cleaned the toilets and bathtubs, as long as they were clean. We realized that it was most important for us to use our time for high-quality activities like being with our families, rather than the tasks that could be done better and more efficiently by someone else. We were fortunate to be in a position to outsource some of these responsibilities and don't take that ability for granted.

If you feel guilty about spending your hard-earned money to get extra help, stop. You might want to adopt a perspective similar to Susan Tardanico's: "If I were going to do this again, I would hire domestic help. I had a set of limiting beliefs about what good parenting looked like. If I didn't do it all—the grocery shopping, the errands, the cleaning, the cooking—I was failing as a mom. I really hemmed myself in, and it took a toll on me and the family. If I had stepped back and run my family like a business, I would have added more human capital." Susan reflects that we are too quick to judge ourselves by others' standards and too easily convinced we need to hold everything together. "We need to give ourselves a break and allow some latitude to redefine what it means to be a good mother," she says. Amen to that.

Even when women are able to get help for some of the home-front jobs, however, life isn't always smooth. The smallest glitch for a child can become an important challenge for her mother—but every challenge can be met with ingenuity and intent, and every challenge can be rewarded in kind. Rosalie, the university president, remembers one day when her daughter was a toddler. "My daughter was in nursery school and had tears in her eyes. She said, 'Mom, I need buttons the color of my eyes for a project at nursery school.' My mother used to have a box of buttons, but I didn't. So I looked down at my brand-new coat and ripped off the buttons and gave them to her. I was actually interviewing for a new job that day and, as I was leaving the interview, the person I was interviewing with said, 'You don't have buttons on your jacket.' I explained to him what had happened, and he said, 'Remember I said we liked you and wanted to hire you but needed to go through the process? Well, I've just decided I'm going to hire you.' My parenting decision to prioritize my child was actually a positive that day."

Working for people who value the commitment of working mothers can be a game changer for women and for the organization for which they work. Susana Marin, the luxury hotel managing director, recommends that organizations need to listen to understand. "Women are very honest when they communicate. If you listen to your women team members, the answers and solutions are there. They can help you organize better than anyone else. My 25 years of experience in hotels have shown me that mothers (especially single moms) will give you the best loyalty if you help them with their balance. Hire someone you believe in and help them give their best, and you will always win. The commitment these women bring is well worth the time away for maternity leave."

To say Dana Born found strong support when she returned to work at the Pentagon after six weeks of maternity leave is an understatement. Because her daughter was in the Pentagon's onsite daycare center, she was able to continue breastfeeding. "When I needed to pump my breast milk, there was no space for nursing mothers. My boss had the only closed-door office in our section and would say, 'Dana, just let me know when I need to go to the gym today,' and he let me use his office. Today they have wonderful facilities for nursing mothers; however, back then I was fortunate to work for a boss who created a facility whenever I needed it," she says. She still marvels at the level of care in her boss's unwavering support. "He'd let me put my breast milk in his personal fridge alongside his soft drinks, and then remind me to take it with me at the end of the day. He was great."

Drop out or power down? If you haven't yet faced that decision, you may be approaching it in the coming years. Given what you've learned from this chapter, let's take a look at what may work best for you.

EXERCISE: MY SURVIVAL GUIDE

Whether you are responsible for childcare or eldercare, you are faced with many demands on your time that may lead you to decide to drop out of the workforce against your own desires. Use the table in this section (or use your journal) to create your own survival guide for figuring out how you can best power down rather than dropping out if that is your preference. We've included two examples to help you get started.

TYPICAL TASKS	AM I DOING IT ALL?	CAN I OUTSOURCE IT?	HOW?
Laundry	Y	Y	Ask my partner to take on half of the weekly laundry.
Cleaning the House	Y	Y	Hire cleaning agency to clean every two weeks.

QUESTIONS FOR REFLECTION

You know the drill. It's time to get your journal out! Ask yourself:

- Have I already dropped out or powered down? If so, what lessons have I learned?

- If I am facing the decision of dropping out or powering down:

    - What do my leave policies look like?

    - Will my job be there for me when I return?

    - Will I suffer from reputational loss?

    - Will my organization penalize me in future earnings?

- How can I stay professionally engaged while powering down?

8

Redefine Work-Life Balance

*Maybe some people will say you can't have it
all. I would challenge that statement and say
you can have it all, but you've got to know what
all means. And all will change over time.*

—Sue Cole, former regional CEO for the
Mid-Atlantic Region of United States Trust Company

In this chapter, you will learn:

- The upsides of having balance in your life and the downsides of lacking it
- Your preferences for the way you bring work and life together
- Some strategies for creating harmony for yourself

Who hasn't heard some version of "You need to have better balance in your life!" And we all know the response: "OK, I'll figure out how to do that when I have the time." Like many working people, the demands on your time are greater than the amount of time you have available. We talked about how important it is to take care of yourself in Chapter 6, and we hope you've done some thinking and journaling to make a new plan for integrating better sleep, exercise, and nutrition habits into your life. In this chapter, we're going to pile onto the already-frustrating load of must-dos that you've been building. And this is our message: "balance" doesn't mean "equal at all times." It really means finding or creating the lifestyle that is *good enough* for you to meet your life goals.

THAT ELUSIVE BALANCE!

The concept of work-life balance commonly refers to a person's ability to meet the demands of work and nonwork roles in a way that provides satisfaction and creates little to no conflict between the two roles.[1] Yet how many people feel they have that balance?

When managers report they have good work-life balance, their own bosses are more likely to view them as promotable. CCL researchers Sarah Stawiski and Bill Gentry, along with their collaborator Lisa Baranik, analyzed managers' ratings of their own work-life balance based on four statements from CCL's Benchmarks for Managers 360 survey, as well as their bosses' ratings of how well the manager would handle being promoted into a new line of business, the same function or division, or two levels up. Guess what? If you feel you have good balance in your work and life, your boss sees you as being more promotable! You don't have to work 24/7 to show your boss you are capable of new challenges. After finding that this relationship holds for managers in both the Generation X and baby boomer generations, regardless of the generation to which their boss belongs, our colleagues conclude that "Work-Life balance is not an impediment to a boss's perception of a manager's career advancement. Managers do not have to give up time with family and other activities they enjoy outside of work for fear of not being promoted at work. In fact, mastering the 'balancing act' might actually improve a manager's chances of being promoted, in addition to his or her well-being."[2]

CCL's Phillip Braddy also found that, in a sample of 2,472 midlevel managers from across the globe (54 percent men and 46 percent women), both men and women report moderate to very high work-family balance without a significant gender difference in their perceptions.[3] Having high levels of work-family balance is correlated with bosses' perceptions that managers are strong performers who demonstrate high levels of competence as leaders. An interesting difference is that women with high levels of work-family balance are seen by their bosses as less likely to derail from their leadership roles as compared to women with low levels of work-family balance. For men, however, there was no difference; perceptions of whether a man would derail from his leadership role was not affected by his level of work-life balance.

THE ROLE OF TECHNOLOGY

The dual-edged sword of smartphones and other technology has had a major impact on our sense of balance. With laptops, tablets, smartphones, and the pervasive accessibility of the cloud, working away from the office is as easy as being there. CCL's Jennifer Deal found in her research that 60 percent of executives and other professionals who use smartphones are connected to work from 13.5 to 18.5 hours a day, five days a week.[4] Even those who don't use smartphones are affected. Almost one-third of those without smartphones are connected the same number of hours, five days a week. It doesn't stop on weekends either! Nearly half of all managers of other managers (49 percent), managers of divisions (47 percent), and executives (49 percent) who use smartphones say they need to respond to their bosses during evenings and on weekends. For those without smartphones, the numbers are lower, but still the pressure to be available is felt by managers of managers (17 percent), managers of divisions (42 percent), and executives (25 percent) to respond to their bosses after working hours. But there also are upsides to being as connected as we are. Communications technology allows us the flexibility to leave the office early to go to a doctor's appointment with an aging parent, a parent-teacher meeting at your child's school, or a committee meeting for an extracurricular board on which you serve, knowing that you can respond in the moment if needed or finish up the day's work from home at night.

Just as technology brings work into our nonwork time and space, the reverse is also true. Smartphones make it easy to take short mental breaks to check your social media feeds and give easy access to family and others who may need to reach you. Yet on the flip side, this easy accessibility can result in spending too much time during the workday on nonwork activities, forcing you to work longer hours in the office or in the evenings at home just to catch up on the day's work. The invasion of work into personal space and personal demands into the workspace can create a sense of imbalance that is frustrating and stressful. Is it possible to reach that sense of balance that seems to elude many midcareer women?

BALANCE OR HARMONY?

Imagine that you feel perfectly at ease with your life. You feel that you are spending the right amount of time and effort on all of the parts that are important: work, family, community, and personal. What does it look like? Are you able to get your important work done in the time period it needs to be done? Are you attending the events important to your loved ones: your spouse/partner, children, parents, and friends? Are you committing time to your favorite charity or community nonprofit? Are you making time to sleep, exercise, and reflect?

Balance, which means keeping two or more objects evenly distributed, is not very likely when we're talking about the full life of a midcareer woman. What can work, according to our colleagues Marian Ruderman, Phillip Braddy, Kelly Hannum, and Ellen Ernst Kossek, is to seek a life that is in harmony.[5]

Women in the middle levels of organizations are very likely managing others, performing functional work responsibilities, and putting some degree of focus on the work of those above them in an effort to demonstrate interest and capability at higher levels of leadership. These multilevel demands and responsibilities often create challenges in how they manage their time. Being ready to respond to the needs of employees means that they can't fully plan what they will accomplish during a given day and will often finish the day with more on their to-do list than when the day started. So "finishing the day" becomes a misnomer. I (Jennifer) remember when I became a manager. I had only one employee to manage, but I also had a full workload of my own and two small children. I remember asking Ellen Van Velsor, my manager at the time—who was a mother of two, very productive, and always seemed to have her act together—how she managed to finish her work and get out of the office each day in a timely way. Ellen's wise words to me were, "You've got to give up the thought that you'll finish everything on your plate. You probably never will again. But you'll realize what is really important to do and focus on that first." It was sage advice that gave me some comfort, and I've shared it with my employees as they are promoted to higher levels of responsibility.

I don't always take my own advice, but I took one important lesson from my manager. I value the importance of shifting my definition of "the work" from covering only the functional work I was responsible for to also include the needs of my employees. I know that a leader loses a little bit of control over her day with each promotion. It's similar to how a woman's life changes when she goes from being single to having a partner, or to having children, or to caring for aging parents. As the demands on our time grows, our definition of "balanced" must change.

STRATEGIES FOR CREATING HARMONY

The women we interviewed recommended specific strategies that worked for them to keep their lives in harmony. A caveat: they won't work for all women. Leslie Joyce, the retired HR executive, reminded us that "there is a complete cadre of women in the world for whom work-life balance is a completely foreign concept. They are working minimum-wage jobs to support themselves and their families, and they don't have the influence or option to create balance in their lives." We agree completely. Leslie was reflecting on some of the women with whom she worked in the consumer home goods industry. We want to acknowledge here that the midcareer women we are addressing in this book will have a greater ability to consider and create balance in their own lives than will those at the entry levels of organizations. The women we interviewed had all made it to the top of their professions. Even though they had challenges of their own, they would all be the first to agree that they had a certain degree of privilege that enabled them to create balance or harmony in their lives. So the strategies our interviewees shared may not be available to all. We will attempt to provide some alternatives, but we encourage you to think about strategies that are realistic for your life and to employ at least one of them to help you create more harmony for yourself.

Start Early

One strategy for creating harmony is simply to start the day early. Dana Born, the retired Air Force brigadier general and current university professor, tells us, "I am an early riser. The first thing I do is make my bed. I'm usually out of the house by 6:15 and in my office by 7 a.m. My 'think time' is early in the morning. I have a to-do list of the 'must get done,' 'probably get done,' and 'probably won't get done yet' on my scope every day." By starting early, Dana can work through some of her to-do list before others begin to ask for her time and attention. Dana also creates harmony by attending to four important parts of her life. "I hold myself accountable for four Fs: faith, family, friends, and fitness. If I'm not paying attention to those, it makes it extremely challenging to invest in my passion and purpose," she says. She doesn't always do all four in equal parts, but she makes space for each in the course of a week so that she is attending to all four priorities on a regular basis. During times that Dana was deployed with the military, her choices in terms of how she created harmony in her life were different than they are now that she is working and teaching at a university. She is now able to put more time and energy into being the kind of parent she wants to be for her daughters. "I've tried to think about how I live my purpose not only in the professional domain. I think about what role I can take that is part of my daughters' human and social development. For example, I've taken the lead role in helping them learn how to drive now that they're older," she says.

Engage Others

Joan Tao's strategy is to get help from other sources when she can. A former corporate counsel and a current manager of strategic partnerships, Joan told us she would advise midcareer women not to "be afraid to outsource the work itself but also the mental load of the work. If I'm trying to wash every dish and fold every piece of clothing, am I more available to my children or not? There is this idealization of motherhood—the person who can make the perfect cupcakes or throw the perfect birthday party. That somehow hurts everyone. You can't let perfect be the enemy of good enough," she says. In Chapter 7, we shared some examples of how to outsource some of the low-value tasks that women are primarily held responsible for. Joan's recommendation would mean that not only do you hire someone to clean your house every week or two, but that you ask them to set a schedule for when the deep cleaning of the baseboards or light fixtures should be done. Put them in charge of making sure that both the routine and deeper cleaning are performed on a regular basis, rather than giving them special requests every time they come to clean.

Be Flexible

As a government minister in Singapore, Josephine Teo realized that the demands of being available to the public—the people she served—put severe limitations on her ability to be present for her husband and children. "My husband and I had known each other for 20 years when I entered politics, so we had a good relationship and I trusted him. He told me that I was not giving the children and him the time that they needed. I had to be very humble to receive his feedback. It's easier to take feedback from people at work than from your husband—it hurt! It took skill and time to adjust my behaviors to address the feedback he gave me, but eventually we reorganized our schedules so that we could have more time together as a family. But we still had to remain flexible. For example, it wasn't possible for us to set a goal like 'We must have dinner as a family together every Thursday night' because there could be public events I needed to attend on a Thursday night. So we accepted that our family has to be opportunistic about its time together because both my husband and I have full, dynamic jobs and our kids are busy. No firm ritual has worked. So instead of identifying a single meal that would always be a family meal, we have committed to get together for a meal sometime during the weekend, which provided more flexibility to work around the ever-changing dynamics of our schedule. And we have committed to spending this time together even if we are missing one person— the rest of the family will still enjoy that meal together."

Integrate

Leslie's strategies are all about integration. One of her favorite quotes is "Beware the tyranny of either/or." A retired HR executive, she shared that she was an early adopter of the concept of work-life integration, when the common practice was more either/or. "You either were balanced or you weren't; you either had it all or you didn't. Having a professional spouse helped me be able to integrate well. Both of us had an understanding of the relative obligations of the other. We'd take car trips and one of us would take conference calls while the other one drove. Or we'd go on vacation and agree we needed to do e-mails at some point during the day and not look at it as a burden but as a way of doing the things that are really important—like be on vacation—and not get so far behind. It gets particularly important the higher you rise in your organization because you're never really off. The higher the leadership position you have, the more people who depend on you, and you have an obligation to them. Just like if you are a parent, you have higher order obligations that you need to accept. To be there for your team." One of the things Leslie and her husband do is to make reservations for their annual vacation "for the same week every year so we were forced to take it. It created discipline around time off."

EXERCISE: WHAT'S YOUR PROFILE?

We've shared a few strategies from the women we interviewed. Some preferred to keep work in its "space" and life in another. Others preferred to intermingle or integrate work and life into the same space. Is one better than the other? No. What's most important is to understand your own preference and to work accordingly. Harmony occurs when you are able to manage the multiple parts of your life in a way that works best for you.

In their book *CEO of Me*, Ellen Ernst Kossek and Brenda Lautsch reported their research on how men and women prefer either to keep their work and life separate or to integrate them.[6] Our colleagues Marian Ruderman, Kelly Hannum, and Phillip Braddy worked with Ellen to create the WorkLife Indicator (WLI), a self-assessment designed to help leaders increase their effectiveness on and off the job.[7]

The WLI is composed of three factors: behaviors, identity, and control. *Behaviors* are the degree to which you combine or separate your work and family life. *Identity* is the degree to which you identify with and invest yourself in your work and family roles. *Control* is the degree to which you feel in control of how you manage the boundaries between your work and personal life. We have made a one-time use of the WLI available to you at no additional cost through the URL www.kicksomeglass.com/wli.

After you complete the WLI, you receive a report that explains your preferences. You will learn whether you are an Integrator, a Separator, a Work Firster, a Family Firster, or a Cycler. The descriptions below are from the WLI report.

- Integrators blend work and personal tasks and commitments. They allow work to interrupt family time or family to interrupt work time, or both.

- Separators keep work and personal tasks and commitments separated into defined blocks of time. They like to focus on work when on work time, and family when on family time.

- Work Firsters allow work to interrupt family. These are the people who are actively involved with business calls, texts, or e-mails at sporting events or on vacation.

- Family Firsters allow family to interrupt work, but do not allow work to interrupt family time. They use technology to stay connected with family while at work.

- Cyclers switch back and forth between cycles of either highly integrating family and work followed by periods of intentionally separating them.

You will also learn through the Identities factor in the WLI whether you primarily identify yourself through your work roles, your family roles, are balanced across both work and family roles, or through a focus on something other than work and family. And you'll learn how much control you feel you have over the way you manage your own boundaries. Having a high sense of boundary control is always more satisfactory for leaders.

How can you use what you learn from the WLI about your behaviors, identity, and boundary control? Once you understand your preferences, you can flex your work style to be more reflective of how you actually function on a day-to-day basis rather than an idealized version of what you think you should be doing. Or you may find the information validating and choose to keep doing what you're doing. A few examples will help you understand how this can be helpful.

I (Portia), for example, am an integrator. I blend my work and personal commitments. I may schedule doctor's appointments or pay bills during lunch hours. If I can't take my daughter to a doctor's appointment, our nanny will take her to the doctor and then Skype me while I'm at work so I can speak with the doctor. I may respond to work e-mails while watching my son's basketball game, or while on vacation I might set aside an hour each morning to respond to the most critical calls and e-mails. This integrator style preference doesn't work for everyone, but it works for me. If I had low boundary control, I wouldn't be able to manage the integration of work and life, and I would feel frustrated and stressed.

Deb, the CEO of a craft and novelty item company, is a separator. She believes in strongly compartmentalizing and separating work from home. When her kids were younger she'd work late during the week so she could devote her weekends to her family. Weekends were her time to recharge and relax. If her job required her to be responsive to work requests in the evenings and weekends, work would creep into her family time and frustrate her.

Michelle Gethers-Clark, the regional CEO of an international organization that funds nonprofits, was formerly an integrator and an occasional work-firster, but a child's health crisis and diagnosis with a learning difference were her wake-up calls. "I was mentally exhausted. I had dietary issues. I had sleep issues. I had guilt. I realized work was taking up too much of my time. I needed to decide what was important," she says. Michelle stopped working on the weekends to focus on recharging her batteries and on her family. "I decided that Saturday is a vacation day. I get up and go to the farmers market. I do what Michelle wants to do. Vacation is a state of mind. I can't enjoy my life if I'm doing what others want me to do all of the time. I don't do laundry on weekends (I get it done during the week), but I will cook most Sundays. I don't do my nails on the weekend. Who gets their nails done on vacation?! You do it before vacation. When I see a woman who is stressing, I ask, 'What day is your day off?' Take a vacation every single week, and you will experience peace and harmony with yourself," she says.

This chapter has presented a perspective of work-life balance. It addresses various ways that different people view balance—or perhaps it isn't balance at all, but harmony. Whether you view it as work-life balance or harmony or something completely different, you are right. What works for you is what is right for you.

QUESTIONS FOR REFLECTION

What does work-life integration looks like for you? What do the results of your WLI assessment tell you? If you are struggling with finding that harmony (and most of us are), don't despair. Grab your journal to jot down your thoughts about these questions:

- In Chapter 1, you identified the values that drive your decisions. Ask yourself: How are my values reflected in the way I spend my time and manage my boundaries?

- Does the way I spend my time and manage my boundaries conflict with any of my core values?

- What is one non-value-added activity I can stop doing tomorrow? One thing I am doing that doesn't create significant benefit for me or for anyone important to me. What one thing could qualitatively improve my life if I stopped doing it now?

- What is one value-added activity I can add to my schedule? What one thing could qualitatively improve my life if I started doing it now?

- How can I hold myself accountable to remove or add these activities? Who can help me hold myself accountable to make sure I am doing what I believe will make a difference in my life?

9

Own the Room!
Take Charge of
Your Personal Brand

*Ask yourself, "Am I mouse or a lion?" A mouse
doesn't want to be seen. A lion is proud, graceful,
and moves slowly, intentionally. Don't make yourself
small; don't move so quickly. Be deliberate.*

—April Miller Boise,
General Counsel, Meritor, Inc.

In this chapter, you will learn:

- How to cultivate your executive presence so you can own the room
- How to construct a personal brand for yourself

You know it when you see it. She has a certain presence. She commands the room effortlessly. It's definitely not just about what she is wearing (though she's always well dressed). It's about her sense of confidence, the way she speaks and carries herself. We've all met these women. They stand out in ways that others don't. When they show up, you notice. They own the room. They have executive presence.

In this chapter we'll explore executive presence and why it matters. And we'll take it a step further. Executive presence is critical, but for it to be truly effective, it needs to be supported with an understanding of who you are: your values (see Chapter 1) and what is important to you linked to your own sense of self-clarity (see Chapter 2). Taken together, we call this your personal brand.[1]

CULTIVATING EXECUTIVE PRESENCE

What is executive presence? In her book *Executive Presence: The Missing Link Between Merit and Success*, Silvia Ann Hewlett describes executive presence as composed of three attributes: gravitas (how you act), communication (how you speak), and appearance (how you look).[2] Among the nearly 300 executives she interviewed for her book, gravitas was judged the most critical of the three "universal dimensions."

Gravitas: Act Like a Leader
If you ask leaders what gravitas means, you'll get a variety of answers. You might hear "credibility," "seriousness," "confidence under pressure." A quick search in Merriam-Webster's dictionary defines gravitas as "high seriousness (as in a person's bearing or in the treatment of a subject)." Executives who were surveyed for Hewlett's book identified confidence and "grace under fire," decisiveness and "showing teeth," and integrity and "speaking truth to power" as the top three aspects of gravitas.

Peter Thonis, consultant and former telecommunications chief communications officer, describes a much-admired former boss this way: "This executive was phenomenal. She had a very quiet way about her. She was charming, very thoughtful, and she never panicked." But what made her stand out in Peter's (and other colleagues') mind was her fearlessness. "She would go into anyone's office and would tell them what they needed to hear." She had earned a reputation for being straightforward, someone who said what needed to be said even if it wasn't popular. When you exude gravitas, people will listen. Your ideas are taken seriously and your power to influence expands.

How do you develop gravitas? Do your homework. Can you stand behind your ideas because they are grounded in data, evidence, or some other base of objective fact? Or do you sometimes "wing it" when you don't have all of the information? Women with gravitas speak confidently because they know their stuff cold. They aren't afraid to take counter positions if that's what's needed. They also have strong emotional intelligence. They are keenly attuned to the needs of others, which means they know how to tailor their message to their audience and what motivates their audience to act.

Communication: Speak Up to Demonstrate Confidence

Women with outstanding executive presence are natural communicators. According to Hewlett's research with senior executives, superior speaking skills, the ability to command the room, and assertiveness are the most important attributes of good communicators. Have you ever been in an important meeting and watched someone lose their audience because the speaker spoke haltingly or had verbal ticks ("uhs," "ahs," and "ums")? Maybe the speaker had a strong accent that was difficult to understand. On the 2016 campaign trail, former presidential candidate Hillary Clinton was frequently criticized for "vocal fry," using the lowest vocal register that makes the speaker sound creaky and hoarse.

Woman are scrutinized for "upspeak," the habit of raising one's inflection at the end of a sentence, which can make the speaker sound unsure or inexperienced. An emerging finding from a CCL research study indicates that men and women entrepreneurs are judged differently in the pacing and pausing of their speech when they are making pitches for venture capital funding. For men, their pace and the ratio of pausing to talking had no impact on whether they received venture funding, but for women, the faster they spoke and the fewer pauses they used, the more likely they were to get venture capital funding.[3] The researchers, Marian Ruderman, Katya Fernandez, and Debra Cancro, caution that they do not yet know whether this finding translates beyond people who are making pitches to obtain venture capital funding.

Fair or not, you are being judged by how you speak and sound to your audience. When we met Nicole, we were immediately impressed by her energy. At our first coaching session she revealed that she had applied for multiple senior management positions in and outside her company. She always made it as a finalist but was never offered the job. She felt frozen in middle management; her dream of becoming a senior leader seemed to elude her. What was going on? On paper, Nicole was a dream candidate. She had over 17 years in customer experience, deep management experience, and an advanced degree. She frequently asked for feedback after interviews and had studiously worked to shore up developmental areas. Nicole was perplexed as to why she wasn't getting job offers.

One consistent piece of feedback Nicole received was her need to improve her executive presence. But what did that mean? Over the years, Nicole had markedly improved her professional appearance and was presenting a very polished image. But there was something else. We noticed that when Nicole spoke, she had a strong rural Southern accent that was sometimes difficult to understand. Her accent was at odds with her sleek, polished image. Nicole is an African American woman, and we hypothesized that perhaps colleagues and prospective employers were hesitant to give her this crucial feedback for fear of insulting her. In the litigious American workplace, professionals are particularly wary of doing or saying something that can be misconstrued as discriminatory. Therefore, professionals of color (like Nicole) may not get as much direct feedback as their peers, feedback that can help them work on particular developmental needs.

We suggested she hire a voice coach to help her with her diction and elocution. Now, we weren't suggesting she erase her Southern accent completely. We probed Nicole to make sure she was comfortable with the suggestion. We didn't want her to believe that she had to be or sound like someone else to succeed. We explored the ways in which her accent might be getting in the way of her having the career she wanted. She drew her own conclusions that minor tweaks to her diction and elocution might help her sound more professional. Over the course of several months she worked with a voice coach, recording herself so she could hear how she sounded. Her hard work paid off. The next time Nicole interviewed for a job, she was not only a finalist but was offered the position!

Nicole is a great example of the subtle and not so subtle impact communication can have on one's career. CCL's CEO, John Ryan, shared this thought based on his work with thousands of men and women during his Navy career, his role as president of the SUNY university system, and at CCL: "If you don't show positive energy and interest in your communication when you are one of 30 or 50 peers in the early phases of your career, you're not going to stand out and you won't move up."

How can you make sure your communication style serves you well? For starters, practice your presentation in front of trusted colleagues and ask for their feedback. Ask them to hit you with tough questions you may receive during your presentation. Periodically take advantage of presentation and media training to help you shore up areas where you need a little help or want to improve.

Finally, many of the women we coach are afraid to speak up during meetings. "How do I get over my fear of speaking up in meetings?" is one of the most common questions we answer during our speaking engagements. If this is you, you're not alone. Nor do you need to address it alone. Tim Rice, a retired hospital CEO, has worked with many strong women during his career. He shared a story about a member of his senior team who had a smaller physical presence and a weaker voice and would "shut down in a conversation. Two hours later she'd come into my office and say, 'I didn't say it in the meeting but what I wanted to say was . . .' From then on, I'd call on her in meetings and say, 'I can tell you have something to say, and I want to hear it. This is a safe environment—you can speak out.' My teams had 6 to 10 people on them, and I spent a lot of time trying to understand styles and strengths. If we were having a discussion and I wanted to make sure we were getting the diversity of input we needed, I'd reach out to those with a quieter voice rather than let the conversation be controlled by the dominant voices in the room." Following that example, one tactic for overcoming your reluctance to speak at meetings would be to find a person on the team or in the discussion who has a stronger voice or more influence and ask them to call on you when you are being quiet and not contributing. You can't own the room unless you are participating in the conversation!

The futurist Bob Johansen tells us to expose ourselves to what we fear, what he calls "voluntary fear exposure."[4] The more we do this, the less scary we find it and the more adept we become in similar circumstances. One simple trick to getting over the fear of speaking up in meetings is to study the meeting agenda and readings and prepare a few advance talking points you can make. Think about how you can underscore or build on a previously made comment. And always remember that when you sit quietly in a meeting, your organization and colleagues can't benefit from the knowledge you bring. Your comments and observations may be just what are needed to advance a major idea, deter a bad decision, or create consensus. Don't sell yourself short!

Appearance: Dress for the Role You Want

Typically, when we talk about executive presence, appearance is often among the first things mentioned. As we've been discussing in this chapter and as we saw in Nicole's story, executive presence is far more than just how you look. That said, appearance matters, and women's appearance can be judged (unfairly) quite harshly. Hewlett's survey results of senior executives listed top aspects of appearance for women as "being polished and groomed," "physically attractive, fit, and slim," and "simple, stylish clothes that position you for your next job." It annoys both of us that we feel the need to talk about appearance when you are trying to Kick Some Glass, but the fact is that appearance affects people's perceptions of leaders, and others' perceptions must be part of your reality if they play a role in your leadership success.

Keep in mind that what is considered professional and appropriate attire varies wildly from industry to industry and from culture to culture. If you work in creative industries such as public relations, advertising, or media (industries that tend to be quite fashion forward), you may have more leeway in what you wear. We find in Latin America and Asia that executives tend to be dressier than our more laid-back American colleagues.

Are you striving to be an executive chef at a top restaurant? You can probably get away with sleeve tattoos and piercings. But that same look will likely hinder your ascent in more conservative environments. If you work in more conservative fields like finance or law, you may find your sartorial options more limited, but you can still use your dress to reflect your personality while fitting within the norms of your environment.

Think of your wardrobe as a signifier of who you are and what you represent. Look for models to emulate within your own industry, but don't be afraid to carve your own path. Think about what you want people to say about you. What you wear should be consistent with your brand. In a previous chapter we introduced you to Jabu Dayton, an HR consultant to start-ups. Jabu wants you to know she's not your typical HR consultant, so she dresses the part: expensive jeans, crisp T-shirts, and unique footwear—a look consistent with the industry in which she works.

Dress for Your Audience

If you are unsure of where to start in terms of appearance and dress, it's always a good idea to look at the most senior women in your organization to get a sense of what is culturally acceptable and go from there.

Peter Thonis puts it more bluntly: "If you dress like you are going to a nightclub, if you are not dressed like a senior executive, you will not be treated like one." A female employee approached him one day and asked, "Do you think I'm director material?" Most men don't want to touch this kind of question. Peter asked her, "How does Mary dress on the thirty-ninth floor? What does that tell you? You have to dress for your audience."

We agree with Peter and know that especially in client-facing roles (think professional services or sales professions), appearance means a lot. You are representing the company, and therefore, you will (silently or not) be judged by how well you represent your employer to clients. If the leadership in your company does not believe you look (and sound) the part, your career advancement opportunities may be severely limited. You may not like it, but that's reality.

Tim Rice, a retired hospital CEO, says he has had to coach some women he worked with in terms of appearance. "I've had to counsel women about inappropriate attire. Nonprofessional appearance. But I'd usually go to another woman and ask her to speak to the woman because I don't think it's appropriate for me to go to a young woman and tell her she's dressing provocatively and inappropriate for the workplace. I think that remark should come from another woman."

Regardless of industry, good grooming is a must for any professional woman. Think about what you need to do to look and feel your best. You may be low-maintenance, only getting periodic hair trims and color treatments. Or you may be more like me (Portia)—I am a bit of a beauty junkie and love manicures, pedicures, and regularly get my hair professionally styled. The point we're making is simply that you should do what you need to do to be viewed in a way that aligns with your values and career aspirations and helps you feel like the best version of yourself.

Consider Your Weight

In this discussion about appearance, we have to say a few words about body weight. Many of our female coaching clients have struggled with their weight at some point in their lives. It's an unfortunate reality that there is significant bias against people who are obese.[5] We started this section acknowledging that women are scrutinized closely on their appearance. Even though the scrutiny is unfair, it's in your best interest to be as healthy and fit as you possibly can be, not just for appearance's sake but for your overall health and well-being. If you are struggling with leading a healthy lifestyle, review Chapter 6.

Wherever you fall in the body weight range, make sure your appearance aligns with how you want to be perceived. Ask yourself, what is the image I want to convey? Do I show up in a way that aligns with my aspirations, or do aspects of my executive presence hold me back?

Amp Up Your Appearance

You can make a big change in how you are perceived with some small changes in your appearance (if that's what you want to do). Here are some ideas:

Take time out for regular grooming. It's the little things that often get noticed the most, so take time out to get your nails done. Freshen your hair color (if you color your hair) and keep your haircut tidy. You won't believe how much better you'll feel to take just a few moments to yourself.

Invest in a stylist and tailor. You may not be able to invest in a personal stylist, but with online clothing subscription services, you can have the benefits of a stylist without breaking the bank, and all delivered to your home or office! Take advantage of the free wardrobe consulting offered by high-end department stores. If you are struggling with your personal style or just want to update your image to be more reflective of who you are today, working with a stylist for a few hours to help you edit your closet and put together a few outfits you can use as a wardrobe guide can be tremendously helpful. A good tailor can make even modestly priced clothing look customized by expertly fitting it to your shape.

Make time for exercise. Not only is it good for you, you'll feel better about yourself and that confidence will show. All of the executives we interviewed have a fitness regimen they swear by. Your exercise routine is an insurance policy against stress and illness. It will improve your sense of well-being and overall health in the long run. Invest in yourself.

THE "B" WORD

One aspect of executive presence is being assertive and having conviction in what you say and how you behave. When this strength is overplayed, women may hear themselves being called the "B" word—bossy. In 2014, Sheryl Sandberg and Anna Maria Chavez, along with the LeanIn Foundation and the Girl Scouts organizations they lead, established a campaign called "Ban Bossy," aimed at encouraging girls to see themselves as leaders by banning the use of the term "bossy" to describe girls' leadership behaviors. The Ban Bossy website states, "When a little boy asserts himself, he's called a 'leader.' Yet when a little girl does the same, she risks being branded 'bossy.' Words like bossy send a message: don't raise your hand or speak up. By middle school, girls are less interested in leading than boys—a trend that continues into adulthood. Together we can encourage girls to lead."[6]

Our CCL colleagues Cathleen Clerkin, Christine Crumbacher, Julia Fernando, and Bill Gentry designed an empirical research study to learn how the concept of "bossy" applied to women in the workplace.[7] They surveyed 100 men and 101 women to understand their experience of the word "bossy" in the workplace. Six descriptions of what bossy behavior looks like emerged:

- Bossy people control others and dictate orders.

- Bossy people ignore others' perspectives.

- Bossy people are rude and pushy toward others.

- Bossy people micromanage and prescribe specific actions (e.g., saying exactly how or when something should be done).

- Bossy people are focused on authority, power, and status.

- Bossy people interact in aggressive ways.

None of these descriptions are what we mean by "own the room!" We mean assertiveness and clear confidence. Our colleagues therefore noted that the term "assertive" was mentioned only twice in 201 descriptors, and even then it was used to describe when someone was not being effectively assertive. So the first conclusion our colleagues made was that bossiness was *not* related to assertiveness. Yet women (33%) were twice as likely to have been called bossy at work versus men (17%). Although the survey respondents said that both men and women have less positive reputations if they are perceived as bossy, bossy women coworkers are rated as less popular and less likely to have successful careers in the future than bossy men coworkers.

Armed with this information, our colleagues then analyzed CCL's extensive 360-degree BENCHMARKS database to determine whether women are demonstrating bossy behaviors at work more than men, and to determine whether their behavior has any impact on their perceived promotability. What did they find? It probably comes as no surprise to you that women are rated by their managers, peers, and direct reports as being *no more or less bossy* than men in the workplace. So even though women are called bossy twice as often as men, they are not demonstrating bossy behaviors any more than men are. When either men or women are perceived as bossy, they are rated by their managers as being less promotable. However, women are perceived as being even less likely to receive a promotion than men.

Why do we raise this research when we're talking about owning it like you mean it? Assertiveness and a strong executive presence may result in being labeled with the "B" word. However, the bossy behaviors described in our study were about poor interpersonal leadership skills, not about positive executive presence. As you develop your gravitas, communication, appearance, and personal brand, be aware that you can absolutely be a strong, powerful woman without being bossy.

YOUR PERSONAL BRAND

We all have a brand, whether we pay attention to it or not. Lily, for example, is an incredible hiring manager. She has an almost scary sixth sense for sorting out the outstanding job candidates from the merely good candidates. She is so well known for this skill that she's frequently asked to participate in cross-functional hiring teams. But that's not all she brings with her. Lily is also known for her ability to train new hires quickly, getting them up to speed in their new roles so fast they are frequently promoted in less than one year. These skills are part of Lily's personal brand. People know her brand—they know what to expect from her. Lily didn't develop these skills by accident. She recognized that she had a talent for hiring young leaders. She studied how best to find and keep talented people. She earned a degree in adult education, which allowed her to develop highly effective training programs. From those starting points to now, Lily has actively cultivated her personal brand.

Your personal brand is how you lead and the unique ways you deliver value. Chapters 1 and 2—about intention and agency—are keys to understanding what you value, setting your intentions, and having self-clarity and a sense of agency. Let what you've learned from those chapters help you articulate your personal brand.

Your personal brand sets you apart from other leaders. It's the promise you make and deliver every day you show up to work. There are many things in our personal and professional lives that are difficult to control, but you can control your brand. So ask yourself this question: What do I want people to say about me when I am not in the room?

Vance Tang, a board member, entrepreneur, and corporate executive, puts it this way: "As a leader, I've thought a lot about my personal brand, about what was appropriate and what behaviors don't lead to being on brand. My counsel to women is identical to what I'd say to men. It's really important to think about how you want to be perceived by others, and to leave that at random is a huge mistake." Whether male or female, you need to be pro-active about your brand, which Vance describes as the promise you can expect from someone. "When someone interacts with me, I want them to know what they are going to get. I don't want them to think they'll get a lunatic on one day and a calm person on another. I want them to think that I'm a person with integrity. I don't make commitments I can't keep. That's part of my brand."

Making the Most of Your Brand: The Social Media Factor

The importance of your online profile can't be underestimated. Think about it. When you meet new people, what is one of the first things you do? Do you log on to LinkedIn and read their profile or search for them on Google? Many people do—more than you might imagine. Does the person have a blog? What is she saying on Twitter and Facebook? What pictures does she post on Instagram? Your online profile is fair game. It's in the public square for anyone (including future employers) to see and to make judgments about who you are.

In the early days of social media, it was still possible to separate your personal from your professional online profile. Not anymore. And frankly, at least among millennials and younger generations, it doesn't make sense to separate your life into parts. You should manage your social profile as carefully as your professional image (because it *is* your real-life image). Many managers and leaders have been burned by posting something on their "private" Facebook page only to see the post go viral, sometimes leading to embarrassment or even ending careers. Don't let this be you. Don't assume an expectation of privacy for your online activities. The good news is that social media offers an incredible (and very affordable) way to boost your personal brand. In the book *Leadership Brand* that I (Portia) coauthored with David Horth and Lynn Miller, we offer some tips:[8]

Audit Your Online Brand

What does your online profile say about you? While there are numerous professional services that can help you curate your online presence, you can do the legwork yourself. Search for your name on all the major search engines. What images or articles come up? Are there any surprises? What would you like to change?

Once you understand what your online profile says about you, take steps to curate your profile. First, think about what you want your profile to say about you. Think about your unique contributions, which you identified in Chapter 1. How does your online profile support or not support that view of yourself?

Look for examples of people whose online profiles you admire. What are they saying about themselves? What are others saying about them? What does it look like they care most about? What do *you* care about? How can you build your online brand to support your interests and talents and focus them on what is most meaningful to you? Every time you post online is an opportunity to build your brand.

Get Social

These days, social media isn't a nice to have, it's a must do. One sensible place to start is with your LinkedIn profile. Make sure your photo is up to date and your biographical profile is current. LinkedIn is the most used platform for professionals around the world, so it's worth it to spend some time making sure your profile accurately reflects who you are. LinkedIn offers a number of free tutorials on how to maximize its social network.

Ready to take it a step further? As you think about the reputation you want to earn (your brand), look for speaking and writing opportunities with professional organizations. Many professionals maintain their own blogs where they post articles on their passions. Don't forget about your own company's communication channels. Reach out to your communications team to see if they are looking for blog posts or expert commentary for upcoming events, trade shows, or media interviews. There are so many opportunities for you to build your social media profile and use it to amplify your brand—use it to your advantage.

In life, so much is out of our control, but your personal brand is something you can actively cultivate. Ask yourself, "What do I want people to say about me when I'm not in the room?" Whether you recognize it or not, you have a personal brand, and it's up to you to make the most of it. Your brand is something you work on every day with the choices you make. What you say yes and no to are all reflections of your brand. Your brand is intimately linked to your values and intentions. When you have clarity about who you are and what you want and you align that with your brand, you can truly own the room!

QUESTIONS FOR REFLECTION

Now that you understand why your personal brand is so important, it's time to put what you've learned to work—for yourself.

Think about your favorite brand. It could be a service, a product, a lifestyle, etc. Use your journal to reflect on these questions:

- What is the relevant, consistent value that it delivers to me?

- Why am I attached emotionally to that brand?

- Why am I loyal to that brand above others?

Now, apply your thinking to your personal brand. You want to represent a brand you are passionate about. Consider these points: Your brand creates opportunities for you, but it can also limit your access to opportunities you want or opportunities that would allow you to reach your full potential. You should consciously attend to defining your brand (rather than having others define it without your input).

As you work through the following questions in your journal, go back to Chapter 1 and look at the values you identified as important to you. Your brand should be consistent and aligned with your values and communicate what you are known for.

- What is my current role, and how long have I been in it?

- How strong is my knowledge and skill level in this role?

- What would others say (or what have they said) about my knowledge and skill level? If you do not know, consider asking a few trusted colleagues and even your boss for some candid answers.

- What am I doing very well in my current role?

- In what areas do I want to improve?

- Do those improvements involve knowledge, skills, or something else?

- Do I have any formal data from 360-degree feedback tools or personality assessments that can provide further insights into my strengths and areas that need development? If not, can my organization arrange for a formal assessment?

- What words would people use to describe me and why?

- What words would I use to describe myself and why?

- Am I satisfied with my ability to reach my personal goals and career goals?

- On a scale of 1 to 10—with 1 being "not satisfied at all" and 10 being "this is exactly what I want my brand to be"—what rating would I give myself?

After you have gone through this exercise, you should be able to answer the following questions:

- What is the value I deliver and the unique skills I offer that no one else can?

- What do I want to be known for?

Don't forget that your brand can be aspirational. We are all works in progress. There may be aspects of your brand that don't quite fit right now but align with where you want to be. That's OK, because the best brands are grounded in some truth (you can do it right now), have reach (you can do it, but it will require some effort), and stretch (it would take a lot of effort to make it happen). And you know all about stretch—the more you do it, the more you grow and develop.

Your Brand Statement

Now that you've identified your personal brand, write your brand statement. Think of it as your personal tagline. For example, here's my (Portia's) brand statement:

I am a master strategist and a collaborative leader. I am brave and tenacious. I lead teams that solve wicked problems. I bring positive energy to everything I do.

Put your brand statement in a visible spot where you'll see it every day.

Use your brand as a filter for all that you do. Use it to guide your decisions about what you will and won't do. What projects and initiatives support your brand and deserve acceptance, and which don't? An effective brand is lived daily. Limit off-brand behaviors—those that don't support or reinforce the reputation you want to earn. As you grow and change in your career, your brand will evolve.

Use your journal to reflect on these questions:

- What aspects of my executive presence am I performing well and do I want to keep doing in the future?

- What is one thing I can do right now to improve my executive presence?

- What have I learned about my personal brand? How well is it serving me?

Pay It Forward

You are fine just the way you are. Do what makes you happy. You don't need to always fit in and do what others expect of you. It's OK to pursue what you enjoy.

—Kecia Thomas, Sr. Associate Dean,
University of Georgia

In this chapter, you will learn:

- Some of the barriers that keep girls from seeing themselves as leaders
- A few solutions to break down those barriers
- What you can do to grow leadership capability in the next generation of women

Pay it forward—this is how we change things for the girls who
follow.

You've worked through the first nine chapters of *Kick Some
Glass* to accelerate your own leadership journey. This chapter asks
you to think about the next generation of women leaders, and to
focus on how we need to redefine leadership so that young girls
are more able to see themselves as leaders.

In 2017, CCL sponsored six Women's Leadership Innovation
Labs in four countries: China, India, Singapore, and the United
States.[1] These labs attracted nearly 250 people, most of whom were
career women but also some men interested in improving the context of leadership around the world for women and girls. To these
groups we posed this question: How do you define leadership?

We asked our groups the question two ways. First, we asked for
attributes of leadership that they would get rid of if they wanted
to redefine leadership in a way that was more gender balanced.
Then we asked what qualities and experiences they would prefer
to use to define leadership. Across cultures, the responses were
fairly consistent. The attributes they told us they'd most like to
disassociate from the term "leadership" included:

- Physical characteristics such as age, gender, and attractive-
  ness

- Ideas that the leader is always right

- Power attributes such as being dominant, aggressive,
  and loud

- Assumptions that a leader can't be emotional

- Beliefs that leaders have a certain personality profile

- Expectations that leaders must work very long hours and
  sacrifice their family for work

The attributes they wish would come to mind when we think of
leadership are:

- Collective attributes such as team oriented, inclusive, and collaborative

- Emotional intelligence attributes such as empathy, resilience, and authenticity

- Strength in business skills such as business acumen, ability to grow talent, ability to achieve results

- Strength in "soft" skills such as listening, empowering others, and compassion

- Strength in innovation, problem solving, and networking

Here's an interesting and quick exercise: go online and search images for the term "manager." Try "leader." Now "CEO." What do you see in the images? When we searched these terms, we saw images of men.

Imagine that you're a young girl, and you're looking at these images. If the images associated with "leader" show men, and the attributes that come up when someone defines a leader have more of a masculine versus a feminine tone to them, who would you think leaders are?

As early as fourth grade, girls begin to see themselves as leaders less frequently than boys do.[2] We are rightfully concerned about losing women in the leadership pipeline when they are already in organizations, but the real work starts much earlier. To solve that leadership pipeline problem, we need to also be concerned about failing to grow and develop leadership mindsets and capabilities in girls. CCL has data from 10 public schools in a single US state where the particular districts are focused on developing leadership capability in both girls and boys. We see very little difference in how girls and boys perceive themselves to be leaders when they are in fifth, eighth, and twelfth grades. There is a small amount of erosion of both girls' and boys' confidence in their own leadership from fourth to eighth grade, but it improves again in twelfth grade. These results are very encouraging—when the barriers are broken down, both girls and boys see themselves as leaders![3]

BARRIERS

What directs girls away from entering the leadership pipeline? And what can you do about that? We suspect you have some ideas based on the work you've done through the first nine chapters. Let's talk about what keeps girls from seeing themselves as leaders.

You're Bossy!

Just as women in the workplace are described as "bossy" more often than men (see Chapter 9), girls experience this, too. Both of us remember being called bossy when we were trying to get other people to do something that we thought needed to happen—like cleaning up our toys, partnering on tasks at school, or playing a game. How many of you remember hearing, "You're not the boss of me!" or "Quit being so bossy!" as a child? We remember it from very young ages—six or seven years old. When you heard it, what did you do? If you were like most girls, you stepped back from what you were attempting to do because you didn't like being called bossy or were afraid of being disliked by your friends. You didn't want to be labeled as "the bossy girl." You thought you were doing yourself a favor in the moment, but you were actually removing yourself from leading. Small instances of leadership, such as organizing a group of friends or siblings to accomplish something, give children opportunities to take on bigger opportunities and roles that prepare them for leadership in the future.

I (Jennifer) remember the first parent-teacher meeting for my oldest daughter, Sarah, which my husband and I attended. Jim and I met with Sarah's kindergarten teacher. I'll call her Mrs. S. We loved Mrs. S. She was a seasoned professional who taught us how to be parents of school-aged children. All of our children had gone to daycare centers since they were babies, so they'd grown up in the structured space of classrooms with other children. Being in kindergarten wasn't a big shock to Sarah in that way. During our first meeting with her, Mrs. S. said, "Sarah likes to be the leader, doesn't she?"

Mind you, Sarah was the eldest of two at that point and had many cousins living nearby, so she was called upon frequently to help with age-appropriate tasks; she was accustomed to being a part of getting things done. But I still regret that my first reaction to the question was to ask, "Does that mean she's being bossy?" Fortunately (she was already teaching us!), Mrs. S. told us that no, Sarah just liked other people to do what she thought they needed to do. Mrs. S. did have some suggestions for how Sarah might go about being the leader in ways that were more acceptable to the other kids, but she didn't discourage her from leading. We learned an important lesson in parenting and leadership that day.

If you are the parent of a young girl, do you see her leadership actions as nascent capabilities and work to develop them, or do you suppress them (even unintentionally)?

I Can't Do That

In addition to dealing with the bossy label, girls also lose confidence in their abilities as young children. A study in 2017 revealed that six-year old girls are more likely to identify a man rather than a woman as "really, really smart."[4] Six-year old boys are also more likely to identify the man as "really, really smart." The researchers then invited boys and girls to play games intended for "really, really smart" kids or for kids who "try really, really hard." Girls opted for the latter, while boys didn't show a preference. The researchers hypothesized that, when occurring over and over again for years, girls opt out of opportunities that require smarts or brilliance, which may lead them to think they are not capable of excelling in certain types of roles and industries. What relationship do you think that has to the fewer number of women in technical careers?

Dana Born, a retired Air Force brigadier general and now university faculty member, thought she wasn't smart as a young girl. She wasn't keeping up with her siblings developmentally, had trouble with physical and cognitive tasks, and had difficulty learning new things. Fortunately, her mom—who was in graduate school for occupational therapy at the time—recognized the situation and placed Dana in therapy. "I was already being labeled as learning disabled before I started kindergarten," Dana said, "and she was concerned about it, so she put me into a summer camp where I had two tutors working with me to train my brain. It turned me around. After that, I still needed a lot of confidence-building because I was behind in a lot of ways. My work ethic set in then, as well as my humility. I knew that without this intervention I'd be on a different track. As I reflect back, I learned that when you pay attention and give care and support, and believe that someone can be more than they are, they can develop to be better than they think they can."

Girls' confidence can be shaken by the consistent messages they receive that they are weak and boys are strong.[5] This happens globally. In their study crossing 15 countries and surveying girls, boys, and their parents, researchers found that girls hear messages that they are vulnerable, their bodies are targets, and they need to cover up and stay away from boys. As a result, the girls withdraw from their communities and the world outside of their immediate family and friends to protect themselves. On the other hand, boys learned to be strong and play an aggressor role. They grow up to have more freedoms than girls have, while the girls are more constrained. A caveat, though—this freedom and higher confidence isn't always a benefit to boys. Boys will take more physical risks than girls do, which puts them at risk for injury and premature death.

A KPMG study found that 86 percent of the 3,000 professional and college-aged women surveyed were taught to "be nice to each other" and to do well in school, but less than half said they were taught key leadership lessons.[6] In your experience, how much more frequently were you taught to be nice rather than provide direction for others? Does your experience reflect the KPMG results?

Where Do I Do That?

Another barrier against girls learning how to lead and be comfortable in leadership roles is that they may not have access to opportunities that would facilitate it. Schools are a primary space in which boys and girls are given chances to lead—leading their class in a sing-along, in walking to lunch or to the playground, or in a group assignment. Around the world, education is valued for boys by most every culture. Education and schooling are seen as the mechanism by which boys are prepared to become the heads of their households, effective employees, and productive members of society. While the same is true for girls in many cultures and countries, girls do not have the same opportunities in areas of high poverty or where girls are not deemed to need an education. Yet even when education is valued for girls, they still may not have the same chance as boys to put that education to use as a leader because of perceptions about what leaders look like or who they are.

Joan Tao, former corporate counsel and now manager of strategic partnerships, remembers first thinking of herself as a leader in fifth or sixth grade. "I had a sense that I was one of the smarter ones in our class, and I had a sense of pride about that. Then that sense was solidified in junior high school by getting good grades and doing well on the debate team. I had ambitions of running for president of the student body. This was when Geraldine Ferraro was on the scene in the US as a vice presidential nominee, so I even had a public female role model. The guy I had a crush on wanted to run for president, however, and he said I should run for vice president, probably suspecting that I might find working with him more appealing than running against him. Plus, he fit the male mold of the president, and I knew I couldn't compete with the fact that he 'looked like a student body president.' So I ran for vice president (and won). And then I thought, 'Damn, I am more qualified than he is!' But that's very typical, right? I knew I could be a better president than he could be. I ran against him the next year and lost by a handful of votes. Even some of my good friends—including girls—said they voted for him. I remember being shocked. I remember realizing that there is something about people not being able to envision women as their leaders."

Girls also have opportunities to learn to lead in other structured settings, such as clubs and teams. There are so many outstanding groups and organizations around the world that are designed to develop girls (we'll talk about these in the next section), but there are still many places where girls don't have access to them. Even in developed countries where opportunities abound, many girls do not participate for any number of reasons—poverty, lack of transportation, lack of awareness on the part of their parents or guardians, or even cultural beliefs and practices.

Jan Capps's story shows how leadership opportunities appear outside of classrooms.

> "I never thought I was being a leader as much as a problem solver," Jan says. "I grew up in Wilmington, North Carolina, in the 1970s, when we had race riots in our high school and community. I was head cheerleader my senior year. We had nine white cheerleaders and one black cheerleader, and we wanted to have more black cheerleaders as one way of addressing the problem. Once we successfully did this, the city council actually asked us—as leaders in our school— to share with them what we'd done so other schools might be able to do something similar."

They Don't Look Like Me

Imagine this: You are a 10-year-old child in the year 2000 in the United States. All of the country's presidents you've learned about in school have been white men. You're a kid, so you don't know much about the political system, what it takes to become the president, nor who all of those other men and women are in public service (presenting much more diversity than the president). You've never seen a woman or a man of color run for president. If you're that girl, or a person of color, do you raise your hand when your teacher asks who in the class will be a future US president? It's unlikely. More often, boys (especially white boys) will raise their hands in this situation because they have seen people like them hold this role.

Role models are critical, not only for women in the workplace but for girls as they are forming their understanding of themselves and the roles to which they can aspire. Unless children have strong adults in their lives who help them see past the lack of role models to what they are capable of becoming, they are likely to limit their thinking about the roles they want to play "when they grow up."

Kecia Thomas spent most of her elementary school years attending an all-black Catholic school. When her family moved to another area of the state when she was in fourth grade, she learned that race matters—she was now in a community that was 95 percent white, first- and second-generation immigrant families. "I heard my new homeroom teacher telling the kids, as I approached the classroom, that they were getting a new student who was different," Kecia said. "I remember thinking, 'What? I'm different?'" But Kecia came to realize that there were few people like her in her new community who could serve as leadership role models in her younger years. It was not until she was in her first job after attaining her PhD that she began to think of herself as a leader.

SOME SOLUTIONS

After reading this far, we hope you're motivated to do something about these situations for girls and young women. You might be the key to a girl making her first steps on her leadership journey. From our interviews, and in remembering our own journeys, we've gleaned some ways you can pay it forward. This is just a selection—we encourage you to find existing opportunities or create new ones in your own community.

Parents and Guardians

Parents and guardians are a girl's first teachers. The women and men we spoke with passionately shared their stories about the messages they'd give to parents of girls and young women. Michael McAfee, for example, noted that it was very helpful for him to be made aware that girls opt out of leadership roles at early ages and that getting girls into math, science, and team sports were all positive steps in cultivating girls' early sense of leadership identity. He now encourages parents to, "as early as possible, create the conditions where their daughters can experience failure and know it's not the end of the world. Help them test their resolve and take that into the world. You can't go into your twenties and not be tested." Michael asserts that girls should experience failure and success outside of the academic context. "It's not just about being a good student," he says. "You can be highly educated from the best schools and still not be a good leader. Academic achievement is just part of the equation. If you can get a girl thinking about that and what her contribution will be early on, wow. You have something really special."

We also heard this advice from the leaders we spoke to:

- Trust your daughter to do more than you think she can—she will usually surprise you.

- Be honest with your daughter that there are unique challenges she will encounter—in school, sports, and her career. Instill a sense of agency, possibility, and the promise of creating her own destiny. Her hard work will pay off.

- Praise persistence and effort more than you praise her successes. Help her learn from failure.

- Prepare your daughter for what she wants to be (her unique contribution) during her formative years. Help her believe she can be what she wants to be *and* be a girl—she doesn't have to do it like the boys would.

- Have the same expectations of your daughters as your sons. Hold them accountable to do the same types of chores, to take risks, and to try hard at what they do.

- Get her playing on a sports team or joining an organization such as Girl Scouts where she can understand what it is to lead and be part of something bigger than herself.

Fathers and other male influences play a special role in girls' lives. Our interviews confirmed what Susan Madsen found in a study of family environments.[7] Many successful women had fathers who taught them and empowered them to learn, be curious, ask questions, and challenge themselves. As Abeer Alharbi, nuclear physicist, told us, "My father was an educator and author in the Arabic language. When I was growing up, he was writing books about geography and distributing them to people in the southern region of Saudi Arabia. He was studying their situations while he was writing about their geography. He asked me to help him in his work. At 10 years old, I was analyzing his data and reading his books! We discussed what he had written. It defined part of my character."

Chris Ernst, one of the men we interviewed, has a son and a daughter. He shared a lesson he learned from his wife that applies to his role as a father, as well as to his role as a leader with female employees. "I long thought that my role when my wife was telling me about a challenge she was having was to solve the problem," Chris said. "In more recent years, I've realized that my role in listening is to help another person feel fully heard and understood so that they then can form a sense of their own next steps—their agency and purpose. I realized that my listening has as much or more power and influence than my talking. I try to do this with my daughter so she can find her own solutions to her challenges."

Vance Tang, another of the men we interviewed, said, "I've never thought about raising my daughter differently because she was a girl. The number one lesson I wanted her to learn was a commitment to integrity from a very early age—and that trait has defined her point of view and has set her apart as an adult. Kids learn more from what they see you do." Vance also suggests traveling with your children to broaden their horizons. "Almost everyone can do some travel, even just across their own state. The more you do that, the worldlier their context becomes. It allows them to have an adventurous spirit."

Having as role models mothers or older women who broke conventional models by leading within the family, community, or workplace was another influence on some of the women we interviewed. Josephine Teo's mother was one of those women. "I was born and raised in Singapore with my two younger brothers. We were neither very poor nor anywhere near to rich—we were considered working class. We had to work for a living. I was particularly close to my grandmother. My mother worked her entire life, ever since she left school. I have never known my mother not to be working. It would be accurate to say that my grandmother raised me in Singapore. I only moved back with my parents when I was 12 years old. So I was able to learn from both my grandmother and from how hard my mother and father worked to support us."

Mentors

Girls around the world have many different interests and needs, so they can benefit from having a diversity of mentorship opportunities. When asked about mentors, most of the women we interviewed talked about mentors they had as adults. But given what we know about how early in life girls move away from leadership roles and lose confidence in their capabilities, it makes sense that mentoring could be important support for girls to help them on their leadership journey. Mentoring can take an informal approach, such as when a neighbor, relative, or teacher chooses to encourage a girl, expose her to good leadership role models, and give her opportunities to challenge herself and take risks. It can also take more structured approaches through accredited mentoring programs.

Groups for Girls

When we asked the women and men in our Women's Leadership Innovation Lab to imagine a future where the news headlines, tweets, and blogs were full of stories about leadership gender parity in organizations and governments, and then to describe what types of spaces would support girls in learning how to become those leaders, they named existing groups (Girl Scouts, Girl Guides, Girls Who Code) and brainstormed new groups that would provide support—such as cross-generational mentoring or connecting girls around the world via social media to encourage and advocate for each other.

We call out a few well-known approaches here and acknowledge that there are too many groups to do them all justice in this one chapter. Such groups continue to form and evolve. With that caveat, the point we want to make is that these groups can make a difference in encouraging girls to consider themselves as leaders and build leadership capabilities. And still there are millions of girls around the world who don't have access to any of them. There is definitely a leadership opportunity in that!

Girl Scouts and Girl Guides

Around the world, the Girl Scouts and Girl Guides organization serves approximately 2 million girls from kindergarten through high school. The leadership opportunities available to girls are broad and help them develop a strong sense of self, develop and practice leadership skills, build confidence and self-esteem, and learn to work effectively as a leader and as a team member. The organization touts that in the United States 76 percent of the women in the US Senate are Girl Scout alums. So are the women who have served as secretary of state to date: Madeleine Albright, Condoleezza Rice, and Hillary Rodham Clinton. Virtually every female astronaut who has flown in space is a former Girl Scout.

Stemettes and Girls Who Code

Many governments and organizations are focused on getting more girls into the STEM (science, technology, engineering, and math) fields. These two particular organizations, founded about the same time, use multiple approaches to interest more girls in the STEM fields. Stemettes is a UK- and Ireland-based organization that inspires girls by "showing them the amazing women already in STEM via a series of panel events, hackathons, exhibitions, and mentoring schemes."[8] Its founder, Anne-Marie Imafidon, wants to promote confidence in girls who show an interest in STEM and to help them be comfortable in saying they are good at math and technology. Girls Who Code is a US-based organization founded to close the gender gap in technology by hosting "clubs in rural Oklahoma, to homeless shelters in Massachusetts, to the country's most prestigious private schools," helping girls everywhere to be "united by their passion to use technology to solve problems in their day to day lives and make a positive impact on the world."[9]

CCL's Efforts

As an organization focused solely on leadership and passionate about helping girls develop their leadership capabilities and presence, CCL has initiated a number of programs around the world in the last 10 years.

Young Women's Leadership Initiative. Initiated at CCL's San Diego offices, this weeklong program brings together small, diverse groups of high school girls from across San Diego County for an intensive experience coupling classroom learning with community projects. CCL has expanded this model and partnered with the Girl Scouts in two communities in North Carolina to offer multisession programs that bring together girls from sixth to twelfth grades to develop their leadership capability,[10] using themes CCL has developed from its research with women leaders: authenticity, self-clarity, connection, and agency.[11] After one of the programs, one girl told us, "I learned that everyone is a little bit different but you can still manage to get along. I also learned that it's OK for your voice to be heard." Another said, "I will use this information to help my middle school and make a difference in the world." It's thrilling to see the growth of this kind of leadership mindset in girls.

Girls' Debate Club. CCL began focusing on debate clubs after a staff member attended a conflict resolution workshop in Uganda. In that workshop, she saw that debating helped women find their voice, their agency. Deemed one of the world's top leadership programs by USAID in 2015, CCL's Leadership and Debate Club program features a two-day leadership training program; weekly "lunch and learn" meetings that feature guest speakers; monthly debates with local university students; volunteer service with NGOs; and three large public debates to provide the young women an opportunity to present an argument in front of a large audience. The purpose of these Leadership and Debate Clubs—which now serve thousands of girls in Ethiopia—was to create a safe, nurturing, dynamic, and self-sustaining space in which young women could develop confidence in themselves as individuals and active members of society. From participant feedback, CCL has found that the young women apply what they have learned at home and that they often share what they learn with younger siblings and parents—a powerful spillover effect that amplifies their development.

PAY IT FORWARD

How might you help the girls and young women coming up behind you? What might you do in your own organization, or with other young women in the workforce, to help women become more comfortable in leadership roles and develop their unique gifts as leaders? Does your organization have (or could you start) a women's empowerment group? A mentoring program for young women? Is there a young woman with whom you work closely that you could develop by using your voice to amplify hers? Women's contributions are often overlooked, so be on the lookout for times that a particular young woman makes a valuable contribution and call attention to it, so that others pay attention and recognize it.

QUESTIONS FOR REFLECTION

Let's get that journal out again and focus on how you can do your part to pay it forward for future generations of women leaders.

- Looking back over school and early career experiences, what kinds of opportunities do I wish had been available to me that would have helped me advance in my leadership journey?

- How can I provide such opportunities to younger women now?

EPILOGUE

If you're reading these words, then you've either wrapped up your *Kick Some Glass* journey or you're one of those who likes to see how the book ends before committing to reading it. We're fine with either one—this is your journey, so do what works for you!

That said, these final pages won't do you much good until you've done the hard work in the first 10 chapters. Don't worry—we'll be here when you finish.

We wrote this book to support and guide the millions of midcareer women around the world who are on their leadership journey and interested in moving ahead but are running into barriers—either of their own making or those created by other people, by their organizations, or by cultural beliefs and practices. Regardless of the barriers they encounter, the end result is that this world has fewer women in senior leadership roles than it should, and the midcareer period is a time when many women either think they've reached the highest level they'll reach or decide to change course. That's why we wrote specifically for women in the middle of their careers.

From the exercises and journaling you've completed while reading *Kick Some Glass*, we hope that you have discovered the strengths you have within you, mapped out some strategies for crafting the next phase of your leadership journey, and found some inspiration that has energized you to take on new leadership challenges. We need more women leaders in all sectors and industries—finance, technology, healthcare, media, entertainment, government, education, nonprofit—you name it. And to achieve that goal, women need to discover their uniqueness, their strength, and their power. In doing so, and with the partnership of men and organizations that understand that diversity of experience and thinking is required for effective leadership, we can get there. We don't fool ourselves by thinking it will happen quickly, but if we don't start doing something differently now, it will never happen.

How will you contribute to this better future?

As you've discovered throughout this book, the answers are within you. It's your job to find and apply them. Because the world needs more women leaders. So let's go *Kick Some Glass*!

NOTES

PREFACE

1. M. K. Ryan and S. A. Haslam, "The Glass Cliff: Evidence That Women Are Over-Represented in Precarious Leadership Positions," *British Journal of Management* 16: 81–90.

CHAPTER 1

1. M. N. Ruderman and P. J. Ohlott, *Standing at the Crossroads: Next Steps for High-Achieving Women* (San Francisco: Jossey-Bass, 2002).
2. T. S. Mohr, "Why Women Don't Apply for Jobs Unless They're 100% Qualified," *Harvard Business Review*, August 25, 2014, https://hbr .org/2014/08/why-women-dont-apply-for-jobs-unless-theyre-100 -qualified.
3. H. Ibarra, R. J. Ely, and D. M. Kolb, "Women Rising: The Unseen Barriers," *Harvard Business Review* 91, no. 9 (September 2013): 60–67, https://hbr.org/2013/09/women-rising-the-unseen-barriers; J. Barsh and L. Yee, "Changing Companies' Minds About Women," *McKinsey Quarterly*, September 2011, https://www.mckinsey.com/business -functions/organization/our-insights/changing-companies-minds -about-women; G. Desvaux, S. Devillard, and S. Sancier-Sultan, *Women Matter 2010: Women at the Top of Corporations: Making It Happen* (report) (New York, NY: McKinsey & Company, October 2010), https://www.mckinsey.com/~/media/McKinsey/Business %20Functions/Organization/Our%20Insights/Women%20at%20the %20top%20of%20corporations%20Making%20it%20happen/Women %20at%20the%20top%20of%20corporations%20Making%20it %20happen.ashx; S. Devillard, S. Sancier, C. Werner, I. Maller, and C. Kossoff, *Women Matter 2013: Gender Diversity in Top Management: Moving Corporate Culture, Moving Boundaries* (report) (New York, NY: McKinsey & Company, 2013), https://www.mckinsey.com/~/media /McKinsey/Featured%20Insights/Women%20matter/Addressing %20unconscious%20bias/WomenMatter%202013%20Report%20(8) .ashx.
4. E. Hoole, J. B. Leslie, S. Bendixon, R. F. Solomon Jr., and R. Eckert, *Green Lights and Stop Signs: The Road to Gender Parity in Retail and Consumer Goods* (research report) (Chicago, IL, and Greensboro, NC: Network of Executive Women and Center for Creative Leadership, 2016), http://www.newleadershipsummit.com/pdf/greenlights.pdf.

5. F. D. Blau and M. K. Lawrence, "The Gender Wage Gap: Extent, Trends, and Explanations," *Journal of Economic Literature* 55, no. 3 (2017): 789–865, doi: 10.1257/jel.20160995.

6. Ariane Hegewisch and Emma Williams-Baron, "The Gender Wage Gap: 2016; Earnings Differences by Gender, Race, and Ethnicity," Institute for Women's Policy Research, September 13, 2017, https:// iwpr.org/publications/gender-wage-gap-2016-earnings-differences -gender-race-ethnicity/.

7. Catalyst, *The Double-Bind Dilemma: Damned If You Do, Doomed If You Don't* (research report), 2007, http://www.catalyst.org/system/files /The_Double_Bind_Dilemma_for_Women_in_Leadership_Damned _if_You_Do_Doomed_if_You_Dont.pdf.

8. Grant Thornton, "US in World's Lower Third for Women in Business Leadership," BusinessWire, March 8, 2016, https://www.businesswire .com/news/home/20160308006361/en/Grant-Thornton-U.S.-world's -women-business-leadership.

CHAPTER 2

1. D. Bakan, *The Duality of Human Existence: An Essay on Psychology and Religion* (Chicago, IL: Rand McNally, 1966).

2. M. N. Ruderman and P. J. Ohlott, *Standing at the Crossroads: Next Steps for High-Achieving Women* (San Francisco, CA: Jossey-Bass, 2002).

3. S. N. King, D. G. Altman, and R. J. Lee, *Discovering the Leader in You: How to Realize Your Leadership Potential*, rev. ed. (San Francisco, CA: Jossey-Bass, 2011).

4. Ruderman and Ohlott, *Standing at the Crossroads*.

5. A. Nin, *Seduction of the Minotaur* (Athens, OH: Ohio University Press/ Swallow Press, 1961/2014).

CHAPTER 3

1. US Department of Labor, Bureau of Labor Statistics, "Number of Jobs, Labor Market Experience, and Earnings Growth Among Americans at 50: Results from a Longitudinal Survey" (USDL-17-1158), August 24, 2017, https://www.bls.gov/news.release/pdf/nlsoy.pdf.

2. H. Long, "The New Normal: 4 Job Changes by the Time You're 32," CNN, April 12, 2016, http://money.cnn.com/2016/04/12/news/economy /millennials-change-jobs-frequently/index.html.

3. C. S. Dweck, *Mindset: The New Psychology of Success* (updated ed.) (New York: Ballantine Books, 2007).

4. M. W. McCall Jr., M. M. Lombardo, and A. M. Morrison, *The Lessons of Experience: How Successful Executives Develop on the Job* (New York, NY: The Free Press, 1988).

5. P. Chodron, "Fail Better: Learn to Lean into the Unknown," *Yoga Journal*, September 2, 2015, https://www.yogajournal.com/yoga-101/fail -fail-fail-better-lean-unknown.

CHAPTER 4

1. M. W. McCall Jr., M. M. Lombardo, and A. M. Morrison, *The Lessons of Experience: How Successful Executives Develop on the Job* (Lexington, MA: Lexington Books, 1988).
2. E. Van Velsor and M. W. Hughes, *Gender Differences in the Development of Managers: How Women Managers Learn from Experience* (CCL Report No. 145) (Greensboro, NC: Center for Creative Leadership, December 1990), http://www.experiencedrivendevelopment.com/wp -content/uploads/2013/11/GenderDifferences.pdf.
3. M. Wilson and J. Yip, "Grounding Leader Development: Cultural Perspectives," *Industrial and Organizational Psychology* 3, no. 1 (2010): 52–55, doi: 10.1111/j.1754-9434.2009.01198.x; Cynthia. D. McCauley, D. Scott DeRue, Paul R. Yost, and Sylvester Taylor, eds., *Experience-Driven Leader Development: Models, Tools, Best Practices, and Advice for On-the-Job Development* (San Francisco: John Wiley and Sons, Inc., 2014).
4. H. Ibarra, N. M. Carter, and C. Silva, "Why Men Still Get More Promotions Than Women," *Harvard Business Review* 88, no. 9 (2010): 80–85, https://hbr.org/2010/09/why-men-still-get-more-promotions-than -women?referral=00134.
5. E. T. Amanatullah and M. W. Morris, "Negotiating Gender Roles: Gender Differences in Assertive Negotiating Are Mediated by Women's Fear of Backlash and Attenuated When Negotiating on Behalf of Others," *Journal of Personality and Social Psychology* 98, no. 2 (2010): 256–267, doi: 10.1037/a0017094.
6. C. A. Moss-Racusin and L. A. Rudman, "Disruptions in Women's Self-Promotion: The Backlash Avoidance Model," *Psychology of Women Quarterly* 34, no. 2 (2010): 186–202, doi: 10.1111/j.1471-6402.2010.01561.x.
7. T. S. Mohr, "Why Women Don't Apply for Jobs Unless They're 100% Qualified," *Harvard Business Review*, August 25, 2014, https://hbr .org/2014/08/why-women-dont-apply-for-jobs-unless-theyre-100 -qualified.
8. W. B. Johnson and D. Smith, *Athena Rising: How and Why Men Should Mentor Women* (New York, NY: Bibliomotion, Inc., 2016).
9. H. Ibarra and M. Hunter, "How Leaders Create and Use Networks," *Harvard Business Review* 85, no. 1 (2007): 40–47.
10. R. S. Burt, *Structural Holes: The Social Structure of Competition* (Cambridge, MA: Harvard University Press, 1992); R. Cross, R. J. Thomas,

and D. A. Light, "How Top Talent Uses Networks and Where Rising Stars Get Trapped," *Organizational Dynamics* 37, no. 2 (2008): 165–180.

11. Cross, Thomas, and Light, "How Top Talent Uses Networks and Where Rising Stars Get Trapped."

12. R. L. Cross and A. Parker, *The Hidden Power of Social Networks: Understanding How Work Really Gets Done in Organizations* (Watertown, MA: Harvard Business Press, 2004).

13. C. J. Palus, V. Asif, and K. Cullen-Lester, *Network-Savvy Executives: Five Advantages for Leaders in a Networked World* (white paper) (Greensboro, NC: Center for Creative Leadership, 2016), https://www.ccl.org/articles/white-papers/network-savvy-executives-five-advantages-for-leaders-in-a-networked-world/.

14. K. A. Frear, A. Gerbasi, and L. E. Caudill (under development), "Who Overclaims More? A Network Approach to Gender and Leader Identity."

15. K. L. Cullen, C. J. Palus, and C. Appaneal, *Developing Network Perspective: Understanding the Basics of Social Networks and their Role in Leadership* (Greensboro, NC: Center for Creative Leadership, 2014).

16. H. Ibarra, R. J. Ely, and D. M. Kolb, "Women Rising: The Unseen Barriers," *Harvard Business Review* 91, no. 9 (2013): 60–67, https://hbr.org/2013/09/women-rising-the-unseen-barriers.

17. P. Willburn and K. Cullen, *A Leader's Network: How to Help Your Talent Invest in the Right Relationships at the Right Time* (white paper) (Greensboro, NC: Center for Creative Leadership, 2014), https://www.ccl.org/articles/white-papers/a-leaders-network-how-to-help-your-talent-invest-in-the-right-relationships-at-the-right-time/.

18. H. Ibarra and M. Hunter, "How Leaders Use and Create Networks," *Harvard Business Review* 85, no. 1 (2007): 40–47, https://hbr.org/2007/01/how-leaders-create-and-use-networks.

19. P. Willburn, M. Hackman, and C. Criswell, "Measuring Organizational Vision Content and Articulation: Testing a Comprehensive Vision Model and Identifying Implications for Senior Executive Leaders," *Kravis Leadership Institute, Leadership Review* 8 (2008): 113–136.

20. D. Hekman, S. Johnson, M. D. Foo, and W. Yang, "Does Diversity-Valuing Behavior Result in Diminished Ratings for Nonwhite and Female Leaders? *Academy of Management Journal*, March 3, 2016.

21. S. Zhao and M. D. Foo, *Queen Bee Syndrome: The Real Reason Women Do Not Promote Women* (Greensboro, NC: Center for Creative Leadership, 2016), https://www.ccl.org/articles/white-papers/queen-bee-syndrome-real-reason-women-not-promote-women-2/.

CHAPTER 5

1. P. Mount, *Why Does a Successful Person Feel like a Fraud*? (video file), July 8, 2016, https://youtu.be/GT_1xv2dk10.

2. P. R. Clance and S. Imes, "The Imposter Phenomenon in High Achiev-ing Women: Dynamics and Therapeutic Intervention," *Psychotherapy Theory, Research and Practice* 15, no. 3 (1978): 241–247, http://www.paulineroseclance.com/pdf/ip_high_achieving_women.pdf.

3. C. S. Dweck, *Mindset: The New Psychology of Success* (New York: Penguin Random House, 2014).

4. P. Mount and S. Tardanico, *Beating the Impostor Syndrome* (Greensboro, NC: Center for Creative Leadership, 2014).

5. "Three Simple Steps to Overcome Your Negativity Bias," Positive Psychology Program, December 3, 2016, https://positivepsychologyprogram.com/3-steps-negativity-bias/.

6. R. Hartley, *Why the Best Hire Might Not Have the Perfect Resume* (video file), September 2015, https://www.ted.com/talks/regina_hartley_why_the_best_hire_might_not_have_the_perfect_resume?utm_campaign=tedspread--a&utm_medium=referral&utm_source=tedcomshare.

CHAPTER 6

1. R. Johansen, *The New Leadership Literacies: Thriving in a Future of Extreme Disruption and Distributed Everything* (Oakland, CA: Berrett-Koehler Publishers, 2017).

2. A. Krivkovich, K. Robinson, I. Starikova, R. Valentino, and L. Lee, "Women in the Workplace 2017," McKinsey & Company, October 2017, https://www.mckinsey.com/featured-insights/gender-equality/women-in-the-workplace-2017.

3. S. McDowell-Larsen (white paper), "The Care and Feeding of the Leader's Brain," Center for Creative Leadership, 2016, https://www.ccl.org/articles/white-papers/the-care-feeding-of-the-leaders-brain/.

4. A. Huffington, "How to Succeed? Get More Sleep," TED talk, 2010, https://www.ted.com/talks/arianna_huffington_how_to_succeed_get_more_sleep/transcript.

5. National Sleep Foundation, "How Much Sleep Do We Really Need?" 2017, https://sleepfoundation.org/excessivesleepiness/content/how-much-sleep-do-we-really-need-0.

6. C. Clerkin, M. Ruderman, E. Svetieva (white paper). "Tired at Work: A Roadblock to Effective Leadership," Center for Creative Leadership, 2017, https://www.ccl.org/wp-content/uploads/2017/11/Tired-at-Work-Roadblock-to-effective-leadership-white-paper.pdf.

7. Working Mother Research Institute, "Moms@Work: The Working Mother Report," 2015, https://www.workingmother.com/momswork.

8. Andy R. Eugene and Jolanta Masiak, "The Neuroprotective Aspects of Sleep," National Institutes of Health, 2015, https://www.ncbi.nlm.nih.gov/pmc/articles/PMC4651462/.

9. Swami Prabhavananda and Frederick Manchester, trans., *The Upanishads: Breath of the Eternal: The Principal Texts Selected and Translated from the Original Sanskrit* (New York: Signet Classics, 2002).

10. Julia Cameron, *The Artist's Way: A Spiritual Path to Higher Creativity* (New York: Penguin Putnam, 1992).

11. E. Chowdhury and J. Betts, "Should I Eat Breakfast? Health Experts Weigh in on Whether It Really Is the Most Important Meal of the Day," *Independent*, February 16, 2016, http://www.independent.co.uk/life -style/health-and-families/features/should-i-eat-breakfast-weight -gain-loss-metabolism-a6874601.html.

12. Laura Vanderkam, "How to Thrive as a Night Owl in a World of Early Birds," Fastcompany.com, 2014, https://www.fastcompany.com /3028426/how-to-thrive-as-a-night-owl-in-a-world-of-early-birds.

13. S. McDowell-Larson (white paper), "The Care and Feeding of the Leader's Brain," Center for Creative Leadership, 2016, https://www.ccl.org /articles/white-papers/the-care-feeding-of-the-leaders-brain/.

14. Diane Coutu, "How Resilience Works," *Harvard Business Review*, May 2002, https://hbr.org/2002/05/how-resilience-works.

15. D. Roger and N. Petrie, *Work Without Stress: Building a Resilient Mindset for Lasting Success* (New York: McGraw-Hill Education, 2016).

CHAPTER 7

1. A.-M. Slaughter, "Why Women Still Can't Have It All," *The Atlantic*, July/August 2012, https://www.theatlantic.com/magazine/archive /2012/07/why-women-still-cant-have-it-all/309020/.

2. N. Kitroeff, "Why Are so Many Women Dropping Out of the Workforce?," *Los Angeles Times*, May 28, 2017, http://www.latimes.com /business/la-fi-women-dropping-out-20170522-story.html.

3. M. Etehad and J. C. F. Lin, "The World Is Getting Better at Paid Maternity Leave. The U.S. Is Not." *Washington Post*, August 13, 2016, https:// www.washingtonpost.com/news/worldviews/wp/2016/08/13/the -world-is-getting-better-at-paid-maternity-leave-the-u-s-is-not/?utm _term=.b6a153e717eb.

4. C. Zillman, "IBM Is Giving Its New Moms and Dads Even More Perks," *Fortune*, October 25, 2017, http://fortune.com/2017/10/25/ibm-careers -maternity-leave/.

5. S. J. Correll, S. Benard, and I. Paik, "Getting a Job: Is There a Motherhood Penalty?," *American Journal of Sociology* 112, no. 5 (2007): 1297–1339.

6. M. N. Ruderman, P. J. Ohlott, K. Panzer, and S. N. King, "Benefits of Multiple Roles for Managerial Women," *Academy of Management Journal* 45, no. 2 (2002): 369–386.

7. R. Thomas, M. Cooper, E. Konar, M., Rooney, A. Finch, L. Yee, and R. Valentino, *Women in the Workplace 2017* (research study) (New York: McKinsey and Company, October 2017), https://womenintheworkplace.com/Women_in_the_Workplace_2017.pdf.

CHAPTER 8

1. M. R. Frone, "Work-Family Balance," in *Handbook of Occupational Health Psychology*, ed. J. C. Quick and L. E. Tetrick (Washington, DC: American Psychological Association, 2003), 143–162; J. Greenhaus and T. Allen, "Work-Family Balance: A Review and Extension of the Literature," in *Handbook of Occupational Health Psychology*, 2nd ed., ed. J. C. Quick and L. E. Tetrick (Washington, DC: American Psychological Association, 2011), 165–183; M. Valcour, "Work-Based Resources as Moderators of the Relationship Between Work Hours and Satisfaction with Work-Family Balance," *Journal of Applied Psychology* 92, no. 6 (2007): 1512–1523.

2. S. A. Stawiski, W. A. Gentry, and L. E. Baranik, "Can Managers of Every Generation Have It All? Examining the Relationship Between Work-Life Balance and Promotability for Baby Boomers and Generation X," in *Research in Careers: Vol. 3. Striving for Balance*, ed. S. G. Baugh and S. E. Sullivan (Charlotte, NC: Information Age Publishing, Inc., 2016), 47–71.

3. P. Braddy, unpublished analyses using Benchmarks for Managers data 2015–2017, 2018.

4. J. Deal, "How Technology Can Help Work/Life Balance," Wall Street Journal (blog), October 27, 2014, http://www.wsj.com/articles/how-technology-can-help-work-life-balance-1414382688.

5. M. N. Ruderman, P. W. Braddy, K. M. Hannum, and E. E. Kossek, *Making Your Life Work: A New Approach to Making Your Life Work On and Off the Job* (Greensboro, NC: Center for Creative Leadership, 2016).

6. E. E. Kossek and B. A. Lautsch, *CEO of Me: Creating a Life That Works in the Flexible Job Age* (Upper Saddle River, NJ: Pearson Education/Prentice Hall, 2008).

7. E. E. Kossek, M. N. Ruderman, P. W. Braddy, and K. M. Hannum, "Work–Nonwork Boundary Management Profiles: A Person-Centered Approach," *Journal of Vocational Behavior* 81, no. 1 (2012): 112–128.

CHAPTER 9

1. D. M. Horth, L. B. Miller, and P. R. Mount, *Leadership Brand: Deliver on Your Promise* (Greensboro, NC: Center for Creative Leadership, 2016).

2. S. A. Hewlett, *Executive Presence: The Missing Link Between Merit and Success* (New York, NY: HarperBusiness, 2014).

3. M. N. Ruderman, K. Fernandez, and D. B. Cancro, "Do You Hear What I Hear? Gender Differences in Vocal Characteristics and Startup Funding," poster session presented at the meeting of the Association for Psychological Science, San Francisco, CA, May 2018.

4. B. Johansen, *The New Leadership Literacies: Thriving in a Future of Extreme Disruption and Distributed Everything* (Oakland, CA: Berrett-Koehler Publishers, 2017).

5. B. Lam, *Weight Discrimination in the Workplace: The Troubling Lack of Plus-Sized CEOs*, November 14, 2017, http://www.refinery29.com /2017/11/180380/plus-size-ceo-workplace-weight-discrimination; T. A. Judge and D. M. Cable, "When It Comes to Pay, Do the Thin Win? The Effect of Weight on Pay for Men and Women," *Journal of Applied Psychology* 96, no. 1 (2011): 95–112, http://www.timothy-judge .com/documents/DotheThinWin2.pdf; E. B. King, S. G. Rogelberg, M. R. Hebl, P. W. Braddy, L. R. Shanock, S. C. Doerer, and S. McDowell-Larsen, "Waistlines and Ratings of Executives: Does Executive Status Overcome Obesity Stigma?," *Human Resource Management* 55, no. 2 (2016): 283–300.

6. banbossy.com/.

7. C. Clerkin, C. A. Crumbacher, J. Fernando, and W. A. Gentry, *Bossy: What's Gender Got to Do with It?* (white paper), Center for Creative Leadership, 2015, https://www.ccl.org/articles/white-papers/bossy -whats-gender-got-to-do-with-it/.

8. D. M. Horth, L. Miller, and P. Mount, *Leadership Brand: Deliver on Your Promise* (Greensboro, NC: Center for Creative Leadership, 2016).

CHAPTER 10

1. J. W. Martineau, C. Clerkin, and S. Zhao, *Ready to R.I.S.E.* (Greensboro, NC: Center for Creative Leadership, 2018).

2. Jane Porter, "Interview with Anna Maria Chávez," *Real Simple*, February 2015.

3. M. Leis, "Difference in Leadership Self-Efficacy by Gender"(research in progress), Center for Creative Leadership.

4. L. Bian, S.-J. Leslie, and A. Cimpian, "Gender Stereotypes About Intellectual Ability Emerge Early and Influence Children's Interests," *Science* 355, no. 6323 (2017): 389–391.

5. R. W. Blum, K. Mmari, C. Moreau, "It Begins at 10: How Gender Expectations Shape Early Adolescence Around the World," *Journal of Adolescent Health* 61, no. 4 (2017), S3–S4, doi: 10.1016/j .jadohealth.2017.07.009.

6. KPMG, *KPMG Women's Leadership Study Report: Moving Women Forward into Leadership Roles*, 2015, https://womensleadership .kpmg.us/content/dam/kpmg-womens-leadership-golf/womens

leadershippressrelease/FINAL%20Womens%20Leadership%20v19.pdf.

7. S. R. Madsen, "The Experiences of UAE Women Leaders in Developing Leadership Early in Life," *Feminist Formations* 22, no. 3 (2010): 75–95, doi: 10.1353/ff.2010.0014.

8. Stemettes, 2017, http://stemettes.org/about-us/.

9. Girls Who Code, 2018, https://girlswhocode.com/about-us/.

10. V. Swan and S. Miller, *The Importance of Young Women's Leadership: Our Story with Girl Scouts* (Greensboro, NC: Center for Creative Leadership, 2015).

11. M. N. Ruderman and P. J. Ohlott, *Standing at the Crossroads: Next Steps for High-Achieving Women* (San Francisco: Jossey-Bass, 2002).

INDEX

ABOUT THE AUTHORS

Jennifer W. Martineau is senior vice president, research, evaluation, and societal advancement at CCL, where she is responsible for advancing CCL's global research and evaluation initiatives and its work on leadership development in the social sector. Jennifer is a recognized author and speaker, having published books, chapters, and articles on topics related to leadership development that creates sustainable impact. As a senior executive and mother of two daughters and a son, Jennifer is passionate about improving the context for leadership globally for women and girls. Jennifer holds a PhD in industrial and organizational psychology from The Pennsylvania State University.

Portia R. Mount is vice president and global leader of strategic marketing at Ingersoll Rand, a global diversified industrial company. She spent over a decade as global marketing leader and member of CCL's executive team. Portia is a sought-after executive coach and speaks and writes frequently on women's leadership issues. As the mother to a son and daughter, she maintains an active social media presence, including her blog where she writes on lifestyle and career issues for working mothers. Portia holds an MA in cultural anthropology from the University of Wisconsin-Madison and an MBA in management from Wake Forest University.

ABOUT THE CENTER FOR CREATIVE LEADERSHIP

The Center for Creative Leadership (CCL) is a top-ranked, global provider of leadership development. By leveraging the power of leadership to drive results that matter most to clients, CCL transforms individual leaders, teams, organizations, and society. Our array of cutting-edge solutions is steeped in extensive research and experience gained from working with hundreds of thousands of leaders at all levels. Ranked among the world's top five providers of executive education by the *Financial Times* and in the top 10 by *Bloomberg Businessweek*, CCL has offices in Greensboro, North Carolina; Colorado Springs, Colorado; San Diego, California; Brussels, Belgium; Moscow, Russia; Addis Ababa, Ethiopia; Johannesburg, South Africa; Singapore; Gurgaon, India; and Shanghai, China.

For more information, visit www.ccl.org.